EXPERIENCE THE POINT

the unofficial guidebook to

Cedar Point

3rd Edition

By Andrew Hyde

ISBN 0-7414-3893-3

Published by:

PUBLISHING.COM

1094 New DeHaven Street, Suite 100
West Conshohocken, PA 19428-2713
Info@buybooksontheweb.com
www.buybooksontheweb.com
Toll-free (877) BUY BOOK
Local Phone (610) 941-9999
Fax (610) 941-9959

Printed in the United States of America

Printed on Recycled Paper

Published March 2007

Table of Contents

1
Introduction

ocated in a small northern Ohio city dubbed Sandusky, mountains of gigantic proportions lie on a peninsula that jets out into Lake Erie. This peninsula of fun is known as Cedar Point. Whether you like spinning rides, slow rides, or roller coasters you will find a ride that suits your taste. Not all of the rides are big rides. Over 15 rides are just for the kids. Many of Cedar Point's rides have been voted over and over again, by many different polls, as the top ten rides in the world. Not to mention that over half of the roller coasters, when built, broke world records.

Why Unofficial?

Why is this book unofficial? We offer an honest opinion to everything from the rides to the hotels to the places to purchase food.

How to Use This Book

The meat-and-potatoes of this book is divided into three sections. The first is general information and features two chapters with all the information on the park, from when to go to where to park. The second section covers "inside the park" and much like how the park is the book is broken up into chapters by "midways (or sections of the park). If you are unsure what midway a ride is located on consult the index in the back of the book. The third section offers information on everything outside the park - hotels, the local area, and more!

Experience Icons

Throughout the book you will find the icons below which bring attention to certain things in the text. We like to call them "Experience Icons" as they are sure to point out something that will help you experience the point even better!

 - Something important, be sure to take note it could be a great tip!

 - For each ride there is a "verdict" given. While some rides are listed as must rides, this sym bol appears next to the "must of the must rides"

 - Family approved attraction! Something the entire fam ily would enjoy

 - Read carefully - it's a money saving tip!

Experience The Point: Online

Since early 2001 Experience The Point.Com has been providing up-to-date news and park information along with feature stories and a photo gallery. Be sure to check it out at: http://www.experiencethepoint.com

2
History

ating back to the early 1800s the words "Cedar Point" have existed. For over 130 summers, guests have been experiencing thrills on a peninsula with some of the finest beaches in the world. Cedar Point, known today as the "Roller Coaster Capital of the World", once like everything else, was nothing. In fact, it was just a point covered with cedar trees. And so the history of the park on Lake Erie began some millions of years ago.

During the last Ice Age, a time in which glaciers covered most of North America, Sandusky Bay and the Cedar Point peninsula were formed. The glacier weight formed what is now the city of Sandusky, the bay, and Cedar Point. Over the years the physical make-up of the park has changed. The park used to have several small hills, but due to the ever changing natural forces of the earth, most are not noticeable(currently the area by the entrance to Magnum is the only really noticeable sloped area).

The Cedar Point peninsula houses much more than the resort area. The resort area, which is the widest part, makes up only 1 mile of the 7 ¾ mile long peninsula. The narrow, non-resort land, known as the Chaussee, is home to private housing.

The first legal owner of Cedar Point, and the entire area, was the State of Connecticut. Shortly after the Revolutionary War, due to the amount of land and homes destroyed in Connecticut, a large piece of land (which included Cedar Point) was purchased by the state and given to the residents whose homes were destroyed. The area became known as, and is still called by many people today, the "Firelands."

Did You Know... Having opened in 1870 Cedar Point is the second oldest amusement park in the country!

Jumping ahead to the 1800s, research conducted shows the words "Cedar Point" first appeared in a legal document in the early 1800s. In the year 1836, a man named Alexander Porter sold the northern part of "Cedar Point" (the northern part would be the area where the park is located today) for a price of 55,000 dollars to Theodore Shelton. However Shelton had financial problems and Porter bought back the land for a mere 292 dollars. Just two years later, Porter sold the land to Ebenezzer Jessup and Stephen Hills Jr.

In the year 1839 the Cedar Point lighthouse was constructed, and is still standing today (it is located in Lighthouse Point). Fishing was extremely popular on the peninsula. Alexander Porter divided up the land between numerous private and commercial fishing companies and required them to pay him back with part of their catch.

Around 134 years ago, a small article appeared in the local newspaper which was written by the editor. It described the potential a small peninsula, covered with cedar trees, would have for a summertime resort. He wrote the article in hope that someone who had the finances would build a small bathhouse on the peninsula. Little did he know that in 134 years that wooded peninsula would be more than just a bathhouse. It was to become one of the world's oldest and largest amusement parks.

In 1870, just three years after that article appeared in the newspaper, Louis Zistel, who came from Germany, started Cedar Point. He built a small bathhouse with sandboxes and swings. Small steamboats were used to trans-. port guests to and from Cedar Point.

Throughout the 1880s, Cedar Point grew and developed by adding many other small buildings and attractions for guests. 1897 marked the year George Boeckling came to Cedar Point. He was a businessman who was involved in the railroads and a member of the executive board at Cedar Point until the 1920s. In 1892 Cedar Point built a massive (for the time) roller coaster and called it the Switch Back Railway. It was the first coaster at Cedar Point. At approximixtly 25 feet high and with speeds reaching 10 mph, the Switch Back Railway was the Millennium Force of 109 years ago. It stood at the present day location of Ocean Motion, near the beach. In comparison, Jr. Gemini is only 6 feet shorter than the Switch Back Railway.

In the mid 1890s, Boeckling started to turn the little resort into a major park. Year after year the park's net revenue kept increasing, and so did its capital improvements. The years 1905 through the mid 1920s are considered Cedar Point s Golden Age. During that time period, many new rides and roller coasters were built. 1905 was the year the Hotel Breakers was constructed. In 1926, the Cyclone, considered by many as the "Millennium Force" of the 20s, opened and was advertised as the "fastest coaster." In the late 1920s Boeckling was very ill but still visited Cedar Point and supported the park as much as he could. Boeckling died on July 24, 1931. The year after his death, the park set a new attendance record: 1,000,000 people. With the start of the 1930s came the Great Depression and Cedar Point began going downhill. They kept building in spite of this. In 1934 Cedar Point built a major coaster, High Frolics. In the late 1930s the Leap the Dips coaster, which was built in the early 1900s, was removed because it was badly in need of repair. One of the major additions during the Depression was the Coliseum Ballroom (which is now the main arcade). The Hotel Breakers also struggled because of the depression.

   As soon as the economy started to move in the right direction, so did Cedar Point. Record attendance was seen once again. The Ballroom, which was on the upper floor of the Coliseum, started to book major bands. Once again Cedar Point added more rides. With the start of World War II, Cedar Point started to go down hill once again. The wood used for the boardwalks was rotting. The amusement park circle was being neglected, which gave the park a bad image. Come the late 1940's and early 50's, most of the major coasters were taken out because of neglect. In the early 50 s Cedar Point s condition was so bad that they made very little profit. and the owners were almost ready to file for bankruptcy. Two businessmen, George Roose and Emile Legros, bought the park. To try to cut their loses, Roose and Legros decided to turn the park into housing. Thanks to the general public, who thought Cedar Point had the potential to get back on track, the people protested the housing plans.

   Work started on modernizing Cedar Point to bring it back to it's full glory. At about the same time work started on Cedar Point, Disneyland in California was being built, with many first-of-a-kind rides. Cedar Point's new owners studied how Disneyland and other parks were being built as well as being run, and made plans for their park accordingly.

1957 - Brought many improvements to the park itself, and a new causeway connected Cedar Point to the mainland.

Late 50's and early 60's - Many different rides were built: Dodgem, Cadillac Cars, and the Sky Wheel, to name a few.

1963 - Mill Race, a first of a kind ride, was built near the entrance of the park. For a short period of time it was named the "Nestea Plunge" as the company "Nestea" which sponsored the ride. Cedar Point and Lake Erie Railroad was also constructed in 1963.

1964 - Blue Streak was added: the first major ride addition to the park since the late 30s.

Late 60's - Brought many more additions: a marina, which at the time had 250 slips, Sky Ride, and three rides bought from other parks: Pirate Ride, San Francisco Earthquake Ride and Cedar Downs.

1969 - Cedar Point introduced the Cedar Creek Mine Ride. It was one of the first steel coasters in the world. With the addition of the Cedar Creek Mine Ride came Frontier Town, which offered several rides, shops and places to eat.

The 1970s brought about record-breaking rides and new attractions.

1971 - Pay-one-price admission began (and is still in use today). Prior to 1971 guests were allowed into the park free of charge. If one wanted to ride a ride, they bought a ticket - each ride required various amounts of tickets.

1972 - The huge Giant Wheel opened along with the roller coaster the Jumbo Jet. The Giant Wheel originally was located at the current location of the queue for Millennium Force and was moved near Wicked Twister in 2000 to accommodate Millennium Force. The Jumbo Jet was located on the current site of Disaster Transport. It was removed in 1979 and has since been rebuilt in Mexico.

1975 - Cedar Point Cinema, which featured a huge IMAX screen, opened. Owners George Roose and Emile Legros retired; Robert L. Munger became their successor.

1976 - Cedar Point decided to take riders upside down (three times!) with Corkscrew. Corkscrew is decorated in red, white, and blue to represent the nation's Bicentennial.

1978 - The world s tallest and fastest (at the time) roller coaster, Gemini, opened.

1979 - The Wildcat and Jr. Gemini opened.

The 1980s was a time when the park updated its image. Many older rides were replaced with new rides and the park started to make its progression from a regional park to a park known world-wide.

1982 - Built on the site of the just removed Shoot-the-Rapids ride, White Water Landings opened.

1983 - Demon Drop's first guests were dropped from the top of its tower.

1985 - Avalanche Run (now Disaster Transport) was built and many of the smaller rides were moved to new locations.

1986 - This year brought Thunder Canyon, a water raft ride.

1987 - Cedar Point introduced one of its most unique coasters, Iron Dragon. During the same year, Western Cruise was renamed Paddlewheel Excursions, and the dock was moved down by Gemini.

1988 - Soak City opened.

1989 - The first shot was fired, by Cedar Point, in the still on-going coaster wars for the tallest and fastest coaster with the magnificent Magnum XL 200. Record books and ratings proved that the Magnum was perhaps one of the greatest ride additions in the park s history.

1990 - The 1985 bobsled ride, Avalanche Run, was enclosed, given an outer space theme and renamed Disaster Transport.

1991 - Mean Streak opened as the tallest and fastest roller coaster.

1993 - Snake River Falls was built.

1994 - Guests started to kick the sky on Raptor, which opened as the tallest and fastest inverted coaster.

1995 - Cedar Point's 125th anniversary. The Summer Spectacular started to dazzled guests nightly during the summer.

1996 - A big and fierce bug named Mantis opened as the world s tallest and fastest stand-up coaster.

1997 - Soak City received a major update including many new attractions. Chaos, a spin n' puke ride, opened near Magnum. Paddleboats, named Swan Boats, were added near Wave Swinger.

1998 - Cedar Point opened the world tallest drop tower at the time, Power Tower. A junior version of the ride, Frog Hopper, was added to Jr. Gemini's Kids Area.

1999 - Snoopy and the gang moved into Cedar Point in 1999, and with them came Camp Snoopy.

2000 - The new millennium officially started at Cedar Point when guests, for the first time, started to feel the force, with Millennium Force. Millennium Force opened as the tallest and fastest roller coaster in the world!

2001 - Cedar Point took a little break from building skyscraping rides(who should blame them, how do you follow up Millennium Force?). Lighthouse Point, an addition to Camper Village which offers cottages and cabins, was added.

2002 - A year for both the family and the brave at heart. Cedar Point introduced its 15th roller coaster, Wicked Twister, an inverted, double-twisting, impulse roller coaster. The former Cedar Point Cinema building was retrofitted and renamed the Good Times Theater and is home to the ice skating show, Snoopy On Ice.

2003 – It's hard to believe Cedar Point broke the roller coaster height and speed record once again, with Top Thrill Dragster, at 420 feet and 120 mph. Troika and Chaos were moved near the beach on the Wicked Twister Midway to make room for Top Thrill Dragster.

2004 – In Novemeber 2004 Cedar Point opened Castaway Bay resort near the Cedar Point causeway.

2005 – maXair, the large spinning ride, opened on the Wicked Twister Midway. maXair was the first non roller coaster/non kiddy ride addition to the park since Chaos in 1997.

2006 – For the second straight year Cedar Point added on to their flat ride collection. Skyhawk, the world's largest swing style ride, opened in the back of the park near Cedar Creek Mine Ride.

2007 – "Are you ready for some serious sidewindin'?" Going for perhaps the fun record, Cedar Point introduces Maverick, a mid-size roller coaster packed with low to the ground turns, three inversions, and large amounts of themeing.

Section 1

General Info

3
Planning A Trip

Contacting the Park

The first step in planning a trip is contacting the park to get their offical brochure. In it you will find the most current prices, information on any new attractions, and other up-to-date information on the park. A brochure can be requested at CedarPoint.com

The second thing is to request a Getaway Guide. It is a small magazine highlighting all the key things at Cedar Point which is filled with different coupons. In the past there have some been some coupons for the Cedar Point hotels. Try to get the Getaway Guide before booking a room if possible. It can be requested by calling 1-800-BESTFUN.Note: our **$$$** experience shows that sometimes if you live too close to the park you won't recieve a Getaway Guide, as they are geared toward out-of-towners.

Stay logged on to both Cedar Point.Com (the official website of the park) and our website, "ExperienceThePoint.Com" for all the up-to-the-minute Cedar Point information. CedarPoint.Com is an award winning website. Besides information has park's site has webcams, a blog that gives an inside look at the park, and many other fun online features.

If you have questions about the park, or wish to make a reservation you can call the Cedar Point information line at 419-627-2350. The line is very useful and the people who answer the calls are very knowledgeable and can answer pretty much any question. Be sure to call the number and request the Cedar Point Safety Guide if anyone in your party has any special needs.

Money

Cedar Point accepts cash, check, money order, Visa, Mastercard, Discover and American Express for admission to Cedar Point, Soak City, and Challenege Park. We recommended carrying some cash as many of the food stands do not take credit cards - you don't want to find out you can't get your Dippin Dots because you can't use your credit card!

When To Go

It is impossible to predict the crowds for a certain day, but looking at past patterns it is easy see common trends. Below are some general tips:

- Go early – The earlier in the season, especially during the first two weeks the park is open, is generally very less crowded
- Sundays in June – Most people have family commitments with graduation and Father's Day events, thus creating light crowds at the park
- The first couple of weeks in June (weekdays) are heavy because many schools plan end of the year trips.
- Saturdays in both July and August see the heaviest crowds of the year
- Sundays, Tuesdays, Wednesdays or Thursdays are the least crowded.
- Friday nights during HalloWeekends are generally not crowded. Saturdays, on the other hand, can see very large crowds.

Getting There

Cedar Point is located in the city of Sandusky, Ohio, which is roughly halfway between Toledo and Cleveland.

By Road....

Getting to the Point by car is easy. The Ohio Turnpike along with highway "2" both run through the area connect to Sandusky.

Distance To Cedar Point		
City	Miles	Time
Chicago	295	5 hours
Cincinnati	240	4.5 hours
Cleveland	60	1 hour
Columbus	120	2.5 hours
Detroit	115	2.5 hours
Pittsburgh	185	3.5 hours
Toledo	62	1.25 mins

• If coming from the Ohio turnpike, use the 250 exit and follow posted signs. Drive time from turnpike to Cedar Point: 25 minutes

• If coming from the east on US 2, use the US 6 Huron/Sandusky exit and follow posted signs. Drive time from exit to Cedar Point: 10 minutes

• If coming west on US 2, use either US 6 or US 250. Follow post ed signs to Cedar Point. Drive time from exit to Cedar Point: 15 minutes. Hint: We recommend you use US 2 upon arrival, due to the fact US 250 is a major road and gets "bogged down." Upon departure from the Point, we recommend you take 250 back to US 2, because it is the most clearly marked route.

By Air....

Cleveland Hopkins International Airport (CLE) is the closest large airport to Sandusky. It is located in the suburns of Cleveland and is just over an hour drive from the airport. Sandusky has a small public airport – Griffing Sandusky - for more information contact the airport at: 419-626-8775.

By Train...

Traveling to the Point by train is fairly easy. Amtrak, the nation's largest rail transportation service, has a station in Sandusky, and it is just a 10 minute drive away from the park. Trains from NYC/Boston and from Washington both stop in Sandusky en route to Chicago. Once in Sandusky numbers for cab companies are posted in the train depot (which is a small, unmanned, building).

For more information, such as timetables and fares, visit www.amtrak.com or call Amtrak at: 1-800-USA-RAIL

By Boat...
    In the park's early days taking a boat to the park was the only way to reach Cedar Point. Today, Cedar Point has one of the largest and most respected marina's on the Great Lakes. For more information on the marina see pages 75-76.

By Bus..
    Greyhound Bus Service has a station located in the Sandusky area. Buses stop in Sandusky three plus times a day depending on the season. For more information visit their website: www.greyhound.com or call toll-free 1-800-229-9424.

Weather
    Planning a trip to an outdoor destination like Cedar Point can be tricky but it shouldn't ruin your plans. Most rides stay open during light rain. If thunderstorms are within five miles of the park all the rides will shut down. Any rides that shut down due to weather will reopen as soon as the storms have passed and the ride is safe to reopen. Despite rain there is still so much you can do at Cedar Point. You can see a show, play in the arcade, or eat at a restaurant.

    Ohio weather is hard to predict especially early and late in the season. Remember, whatever the weather is supposed to be it is always a few degrees cooler at Cedar Point thanks to the lake, so plan accordingly. In May and early June the breezes off the lake can make for some chilly evenings, while the weather in September and October can be any where from 80 degrees and sunny to near freezing temps and rain.

    If the weather forecast says rain in the morning, don't change your plans! Most people won't go if it is going to rain, thus creating shorter lines.

Time Needed
    Cedar Point is often mistaken as an average amusement park in which one can visit and take in everything in one day. Depending on the time of year it is becoming harder, if not impossible, to see EVERYTHING in a one day span.

    In general, most of the major rides and attractions can be taken in during one day, but you may still not be able to ride every ride and see every show. If you plan on going on a Saturday during the fall or summer, or over a holiday two days are a must to "experience the point." If you wish to see shows, visit Soak City and/or Challenge Park, spend time at the beach, or reride your favorite rides, then two days is a must.

A popular trip itinerary to arrive in the late afternoon hours, visit the park that evening (taking advantage of the later in the day pricing) and spending the night. By spending the night you can wake up and head to the park refreshed, and spend the better part of the day at the park doing everything you missed the night before.

Another popular trip itinerary is spending two nights - and taking advantage of Soak City. On day 1 travel and arrive at the park in the early evening hours. Take advantage of either the attractions in Challenge Park or visit the park in the evening hours. Spend day 2 at Cedar Point. I recommend that during the day you take advantage of your hotel for a quick nap and to "freshen up." Day 3 take your time waking up and checking out of your hotel before heading over to Soak City. Soak City is not a full day park so you would most likely be ready to leave before or around dinner time - giving you plenty of time to start your travel back home.

Making the Most of Your Time

With a little planning and following some tips you can make the most of your time at the park.

• **Arrive early** - So many people arrive at the park at the listed opening time or after. For the first few hours the park doesn't have as large of crowds as say the middle of the day. The park opens the gates to the public generally 30 mins prior to the listed opening time. Some people arrive before that and line up at the gates to get ready to jump and run when the gates open.

• **The "back"** - Most people arrive at the park and head either to the new ride or a marquee attraction. Many also ride the first ride they see (for example Raptor since it is near where most people enter the park, has large lines in the morning and at night when people are leaving, but shorter lines mid day). Upon arrival, take advantage of the crowd patterns and head for the back of the park. Even on some of the most crowded days, rides like Magnum, Power Tower, Gemini, and Mean Streak generally have short or no lines during the first hour the park is open. Rides in the front of the park generally have shorter lines mid day once the crowds have dispersed around the park.

• **Buy tickets in advance** - Not only is it usually cheaper to buy tickets in advance (see following page) but it can save you time once you arrive at the park.

• **Plan** - Many assume Cedar Point is much like any other local amusement park, when in reality it isn't - its the world's largest amsusement park and has more rides and attractions than any other place on the planet. If you take just a few minutes, perhaps in the car while driving to the park, discussing which rides you and your group want to ride, it will save time once you get in the park.

Park Tickets and Discounts

Cedar Point offers numerous ticket options. Below is a list of 2007 prices (subject to change). Children 2 and under are free.

Funday - Ages 3-61, 48" and taller.	$41.95
Jr. Funday - Ages 3 and older, under 48" tall in shoes.	$11.95
Senior Funday - Ages 62 and older	$11.95
2 day Ride & Slide - Ages 3-61, 48" and taller. Ride & Slide Ticket will admit one guest to both Cedar Point and Soak City for any two regular season days.	$69.95
2 day Ride & Slide - Junior - Age 3 and over; under 48" tall. Ride & Slide Junior Ticket will admit one guest to both Cedar Point and Soak City for any two regular season days.	$29.95
2 day Ride & Slide - Senior - Age 62 and over. Ride & Slide Senior Ticket will admit one guest to both Cedar Point and Soak City for any two regular season days.	$29.95
Cedar Point Starlight - Valid after 5 p.m. when Cedar Point closes at 10 p.m. or later; valid after 4 p.m. when Cedar Point closes earlier than 10 p.m.	$24.95
Military - Valid ID required. Discount applies only to active or retired military personnel and immediate family members.	$31.00

Soak City pricing is as follows (though the two day Ride & Slide for both parks is listed above):

Regular All Day - Ages 3 and older, over 48" tall in bare feet.	$28.00
Junior All Day - Ages 3 and older, under 48" tall in bare feet.	$9.95
Senior All Day - Ages 62 and over.	$9.95
Starlight - After 5 p.m. when Soak City closes at 9 p.m.; after 4 p.m. when Soak City closes at 7 p.m. or 8 p.m.	$15.95
Children - Age 2 and under	Free

!   The biggest tip that can be given is that there are plenty of
ways to avoid paying full price. In fact, we like to think
that there are enough ways to get discounted tickets that the   **$$$**
general rule of thumb is that you should never have to pay
full price.There are many different discounts available all over for
a regular adult ticket into the park. Below is a list of discounts, but
please note the list can change at any time, so use it as a guide:

   • **Pop/soda cans** - nearly every year a promotion is ran on cans of a
certain sode/pop company. The can usually allows guests to get several dollars
off the price of admission if they bring the can to the park (the coupon is right
on the can). The promotion normally occurs in late spring/early summer.
   • **Local "rec" center** - many local (mainly within a few hours of the
park) city recreation centers sell discounted tickets
   • **Buy a season pass** - Planning to visit Cedar Point for more than two
days in a single season? Then a season pass is for you! For $109 dollars a
season pass is cheaper than buying three single day park tickets! While there
is a little work involved with getting a season pass (you have to spend a few
minutes getting your picture taken at the season pass center) you do get put on
a mailing list and often get special discounts. For more on season passes see
the following pages.

Season Passes

     A season pass is pass that allows a single person unlimited entry
into the park for a single season, is a great way to save money if you are plan-
ning to visit the park several times.
     There are three different season passes available: a regular Cedar
Point only pass, a "MAXX" pass, and a "MAXX Plus" pass. The regular
Cedar Point only pass allows the passholder access to Cedar Point and Cedar
Point only for the entire season. The "Maxx" pass allows the passholder ac-
cess to Cedar Point and every other amusement park Cedar Fair owns (which
includes Kings Island, Knotts Berry Farms, Dorney Park and many other parks
- see complete list below). The "Maxx Plus" pass allows passholder access

into Cedar Point and all Cedar Fair amusement parks AND waterparks (including season long access into Soak City - see complete list below). Cedar Point offers a "VIP" program to season pass holders called the Joe Cool Club. For an additional fifteen dollars a year a season passholder can become a member and receive discounts, special offers, and exclusive ride times on certain attractions.

Regular - Ages 3-61; 48" tall & taller. Valid only at Cedar Point.	$109.95
MAXX Pass - Ages 3-61; 48" tall and taller. Valid at any CFLP ride park.	$125.00
MAXX Plus Pass - Ages 3-61; 48" tall & taller. Valid at any CFLP ride park or outdoor waterpark.	$164.95
Junior Regular - Ages 3 & over; under 48" tall when ID picture is taken. Valid only at Cedar Point.	$49.95
Junior MAXX Plus Pass - Ages 3 & over; under 48" tall when ID picture is taken. Valid at any CFLP ride park or outdoor waterpark	$79.95
Senior Regular - Ages 62 & older. Valid only at Cedar Point.	$49.95
Senior MAXX Plus Pass - Ages 62 & older. Valid at any CFLP ride park or outdoor waterpark.	$79.95
Cedar Point Parking Pass - Per vehicle, one non-transferable parking sticker, registered and affixed to a single, non-commercial vehicle. Valid at Cedar Point only.	$70.00
All Ohio Parking Pass - Per vehicle, one non-transferable parking sticker, registered & affixed to a single, non-commercial vehicle. Valid at Cedar Point, Geauga Lake & Kings Island only.	$75.00
Joe Cool Club Membership	$15.00

Season parking passes are also available. The regular pass is available for just Cedar Point, while the all Ohio parking pass allows the car which the pass is applied to park free at Cedar Point, Geauga Lake, and Kings Island.

Listed below are all the parks, and their location, which Cedar Fair ownss.

• MAXX passes are valid at: Cedar Point in Sandusky, OH; Geauga Lake and Wildwater Kingdom in Aurora, OH; Michigan's Adventure in Muskegon, MI; Paramount's Kings Island in Mason, OH; Paramount's Kings Dominion near Richmond, VA; Paramount's Great America in Santa Clara, CA; Paramount Canada's Wonderland near Toronto, ON; Paramount's Carowinds in Charlotte, NC; Bonfante Gardens, Gilroy, CA; Knott's Berry Farm in Buena Park, CA; Dorney Park and Wildwater Kingdom in Allentown, PA; Valleyfair in Shakopee, MN; Worlds of Fun in Kansas City, MO

• MAXX Plus passes are valid at: Cedar Point and Soak City in Sandusky, OH; Geauga Lake and Wildwater Kingdom in Aurora, OH; Michigan's Adventure in Muskegon, MI; Paramount's Kings Island in Mason, OH; Paramount's Kings Dominion near Richmond, VA; Paramount's Great America in Santa Clara, CA; Paramount Canada's Wonderland near Toronto, ON; Paramount's Carowinds in Charlotte, NC; Bonfante Gardens in Gilroy, CA; Knott's Berry Farm and Soak City in Buena Park, CA; Soak City in Palm Springs and San Diego, CA; Dorney Park and Wildwater Kingdom in Allentown, PA; Valleyfair in Shakopee, MN; Worlds of Fun and Oceans of Fun in Kansas City, MO.

For more information visit the Season Pass center (located to the left of the admission gates) or call (419) 627-2309.

4

Park Information

Cedar Point is an experience in itself. There is more to the park than just rides. This chapter answers questions about parking, where to enter the park (there are in fact several entrances into the park), what do to with your pets for the day, and fills you in on all the other, sometimes not well known, policies and perks offered by the park that can make your trip smoother and much more enjoyable.

Parking

Parking. Doesn't sound like a big deal now does it? Wrong, it is. Be prepared to open up your wallet when you arrive at the park as the parking price for the 2007 season is set at ten dollars. Now what if you were told you could get that ten dollars back? Well, in theory, you can. If you stay at the Cedar Point resorts or eat at one of the sit-down restruants listed on the parking pass (if none are listed ask at guest services near the entrance of the park), your parking pass becomes an automatic ten dollar off coupon.

$$$

Another secret to parking is that you do not have to park in the massive main lot. You can park near Soak City/back of Cedar Point. Why would you want to park there? You could then enter the park in the back and beat all the crowds to the attractions in the back of the park. To park in the back simply follow the signs marked "Resorts" or "Soak City." See below for more information about the back entrance into the park.

Entrances into the park

There is more than one entrance into the park. What's the big deal about where you enter the park? The biggest answer would be beating the crowds. Think about it - you arrive around the same time as roughly 70% of the park's visitors for the day. If you drive around the park (see previous page about parking) and enter in the back you just beat that 70% to the back of the park!

Below is a list of the various entrances into the park - all of which are open to the public.

- **Main gate** - Main entrance into park
- **Marina gate** - Located near the Good Times Theatre in the middle of the park on the Sandusky Bay (east side) side.
- **Resort gate** - Located near the station of Magnum XL-200. This gate is mostly used for those staying at Hotel Breakers, Sandcastle Suites, and Camper Village (Lighthouse Point). This is the gate to use if you wish to visit Challenge Park or Soak City.
- **Beach gate** - Located on the far right hand side of the park near the beach, just north of Wicked Twister. This gate is used for those staying at the hotels, but is also the gate to use if you wish to visit TGI Friday or the other restaurants in the Hotel Breakers, or rent ski jets and other water equipment.

If you wish to leave the park at any time during the day, you can get your hand stamped free of charge. This stamp allows you to re-enter the park at any time that same day. The stamp used to stamp your hand IS waterproof (just don't try to wash it off). Try to not put sunscreen over the stamp because that may cause the stamp to fade.

Pet Check

Pets (except service animals) are not allowed in Cedar Point or any of Cedar Point's hotels. Cedar Point does provide a place for your pets to stay during your trip (overnight stay not permitted). Pet Check is located near the Cedar Point Marina across from the bus parking lot.

Lockers and Rentals

Lockers throughout the park range in size(and price). They can be found at various locations in the park: just inside the main entrance (on the right), near Power Tower, near Millennium Force, near Magnum's exit, near Snake River Falls and near Thunder Canyon.

Did You Know... There are exactly sixty-seven pop machines throughout the park - all of which serve Pepsi!

Cedar Point rents strollers, wagons, wheelchairs, and pagers. They are available for rent near the front of the park by Demon Drop. Near the rock-climbing wall by Camp Snoopy only strollers, wagons, and wheelchairs are available for rent. Please be advised that renting is done on a first-come first-serve basis, so we highly recommend bringing your own.

Picnic Areas

Cedar Point has picnic areas both inside and outside the park. The picnic areas are located at the very front of the park. Cedar Point allows guests to bring their own food and drinks into the outside picnic areas only. Ohio laws prohibit guests from bringing any alcohol on Cedar Point property.

$$$ By packing lunch, or even just snacks, you can save a lot of money, as the price of both food and drink at the park is very high. My favorite thing to do is pack my own sandwich, or pick one up on the way to the park and eat lunch in the picnic area or in my car while taking a break from the park. Don't forget to pack drinks (non-alcoholic - bringing your own alcoholic drinks to Cedar Point is against the law) as drinks at the park are not cheap.

Along Rte. 250 near the park there are several places you could stop to pick up picnic supplies. Meijers is a large superstore with a full grocery area and is located just north of 2 on 250.

Parent Swap Programs

Parents are you sick of traveling all the way to Cedar Point and not getting the chance to ride anything because you brought your young kids along? Thanks to a program offered by the park called "Parent Swap," it becomes possible for thrill seeking parents to ride their favorite attractions!

One parent and the rest of the group (who are of the correct height) enter the line. Once the ride is over, the parent who just rode has the ride operator sign off (on the parent swap form) and exits the ride. The parent that was waiting enters the ride, through the exit. That parent may bring one person with them (who is the proper height). In order to enter the ride through the exit the parent must show the parent swap form. So it is possible (and ok) for a person of the correct height to ride twice (once with each parent).

You can obtain a parent swap form at the resort gate, Town Hall Museum, Guest Services, and Park Operations office.

Money Services

Cedar Point accepts Visa, MasterCard and Discover/NOVUS for tickets, accommodations, and at most gift shops and restaurants.

- ATM machines are available in and near the park
- Personal checks, traveler's checks and money orders may be cashed at the Park Operations office (in the main arcade near Kiddy Kingdom).
- Large US bills can be exchanged for smaller ones at the Park Opera tions Office
- Canadian money may be exchanged at all the entrance gates, the Gemini Arcade, the Main Arcade, and at the Park Operations office.

Height & Size Restrictions

Most rides at Cedar Point have height requirements for safety reasons. If someone is under the height requirement, they cannot ride. Cedar Point hires a professional biodynamic engineer to test the rides and find the minimum height requirements. Some rides have a height requirement to ride alone, but anyone can ride if accompanied by a responsible person. Cedar Point considers a responsible person to be someone 16 years of age or older and shows the maturity of a 16+ year old. If a child is close to a certain height mark they can be "officially" measured at the Park Operations office (south side of Main Arcade near Kiddy Kingdom). A child would then be given a wristband showing that they are a certain height, and the child would not have to be measured at each ride.

Guests of exceptional size may not fit into a ride. On the rides where this problem may exist, there is a test seat at the entrance. Also, people with disabilities may not be able to ride certain rides (see the Handicap/Special Needs section below).

Note: Cedar Point may ask a child to remove their shoes if they are close to the height requirement. Therefore, we don't suggest putting things in shoes or wearing high heels. Remember, safety is no accident. At Soak City children cannot be in shoes or sandals when they are measured.

VIP Tours

Want the VIP treatment at the park? Cedar Point recently started offering VIP tours which include a personal escort and the chance to skip all the lines.

The VIP tour includes
- Admission to Cedar Point
- Personal Cedar Point escort
- Exclusive parking
- Front-of-the-line access to all the parks ride
- Priority restaurant seating
- Priority live show seating
- Two complimentary on-ride photos (where available)

Prices:
- $350.00 per person (for parties of 4 or more)
- $400.00 per person (for parties of 2 or 3)

A few things to take note of: The tours must be reserved in advance as there is limited availability for each day. A credit card is required to make a reservation. All tours must be cancelled 24 hours prior to your visit or a 10% (of total package price) cancellation fee will be assessed. All tour participants must follow all park rules at all times. Two and three day pricing is available, call for more information.

For more information, or to place a reservation:
- Call 419-627-2225
- Reservations are welcome Monday through Friday, 8am until 4:30pm.

Park Events

Each year Cedar Point holds numerous park events each year. Listed below is some of the most popular annual events.

HalloWeekends

For over ten year when fall arrives at the park, so does HalloWeekends. Each year from late Septemeber through closing day Cedar

Point is transformed into a park-wide halloween event called Halloweekends. Haunted houses, "fright zones", a fun house for kids, and a whole new selection of entertainment themed around halloween is added to the park for the event. Hundreds of fog machines are added to "fog up" the park, which is decked out in halloween decorations. Camp Snoopy is tranformed into Camp Spooky and even the Peanuts gang dresses up in their halloween costumes. The best part is that all the added halloween attractions are included in the price of admission!

HalloWeekends takes place on Friday, Saturday and Sundays in the fall. On Friday the park is open from 6pm-11pm, on Saturday from noon to midnight and on Sunday from 10am-8pm (with the exception of Columbus Day weekend, when the park stays open till 10pm on Sunday). On Friday nights only the the haunted house, fright zones, and select rides are open. Select rides meaning most of the major roller coasters along with a few thrill ride. Camp Spooky and most other kid rides are closed. Due to the limited ride availability on Friday, the price of admission is discounted. On Saturday all attractions are open (though certain haunted houses and fright zones may open later in the day). On Sundays all attractions, along with all the HalloWeekends attractions, are open (except for the fright zones, but they are open the one Sunday the park is open later - Columbus Day weekend). HalloWeekends can be some of the park's busiest times of the year. Try to avoid Saturdays unless you have a two/three day trip planned, as some of the Saturdays, especially if the weather is remotely nice, can see the park completely full. Friday nights are generally uncrowded and provide a great chance to ride your favorite roller coaster without much of a wait (but again Friday nights feature a limited ride availability). If you are wondering about your favorite attraction call the park at 419-627-2350 closer to the fall when the exact list is available. Sundays are also generally not nearly as crowded as Saturdays, and the lines are quite manageable.

Did You Know...

Over 5,000 individual cornstalks are placed around the park to set the mood for HalloWeekends!

Despite what the name "HalloWeekends" may imply, the event is geared toward both adults and children. Children can enjoy unique shows especially for them, a rethemed Camp Snoopy (for HalloWeekends it becomes "Camp Spooky"), a fun house just for children, and many other events. The park does a good job of separating the really scary stuff from the family attractions. For the most part the "fright zones" (areas of the park which feature fog, scary creatures and themes) don't start up until the evening hours and even then there is always a way around them (which is clearly marked).

Overall, HalloWeekends being the same price as any other time of the year, the extra halloween attractions, events, and decor add some value to the ticket price. Many find the park much more relaxing in the fall thanks to the cooler tempatures. HalloWeekends is a great time to visit the park.

New for 2007, Cedar Point will debut a parade as part of the HalloWeekends event. As of print time no other information on the parade is available.

The park generally releases information for the upcoming year's HalloWeekends' event in the middle of the summer (though the event's dates are announced in early spring). Check ExperienceThePoint.Com or Cedar-Point.Com for more information around that time.

CoasterMania

Cedar Point is known world-wide for its collection of roller coasters and thrill rides – especially among roller coaster enthusiasts. What better way to please the thousands of enthusiasts than throw a big coaster party? That is what's CoasterMania is. Each year CoasterMania is held annually on the first or second Friday of June. The event (which changes slightly each year), draws an average 1,000 coaster fanatics. It normally consists of a picnic lunch, contests, discounts, presentations, and over hours upon hours of E.R.T (exclusive ride time). Uusually the parking open opens as early as 5am so coaster enthusiasts can gather, buy tickets and get pumped for the day adhead. E.R.T starts around 7am and runs until the park opens, and then from just after closing time until late into the night. The event is FREE (with the purchase of park admission and if you have a season pass you pay nothing). So what's the catch? You have to be a member of a roller coaster club (members can bring up to one guest).

CoasterMania is always a great time to not only experience Cedar Point but to meet people from all around the world who share a passion for roller coasters.

For more information on roller coaster clubs see page 93.

Boat Show

Officially called the North American Sail & Power Boat Show, the boat show is a separate priced event held each fall near and around the park's marina. Sponsored by the Lake Erie Marine Trades Association (L.E.M.T.A.), past year's festivities have featured more than 700 sail and power boats, a flying boat, nautical accessories, brokerage pier, party barge and much more. Admission to the boat show does not include admission to Cedar Point. . For information about the North American Sail & Power Boat Show, please call L.E.M.T.A. at 440.899.5009 or visit www.boatohio.com.

Section 2

Inside The Park

5
Main Midway

The grandest of all the midways, the Main Midway at Cedar Point is the most recognizable area of the park perhaps because its roots go back to the traditional style of design of many of the world's other parks. Stretching from the main entrance plaza back to the train station plaza, the main midway is filled with the widest selection of rides, stores, games and eateries. The "main branch/path" of the midway it follows the traditional main street style design - shops and attractions on either side of a large boulevard style path.

Highlights of this section of the park include the roller coaster Raptor, the peaceful Sky Ride, and Hot Potato – the best place to grab a snack in the park.

Rides

Blue Streak

Type of ride: Mild wooden roller coaster
Height Requirement: Min. 48in
Intensity Rating: 3/5

Blue Streak is a classic wooden coaster. Built in 1964, Blue Streak takes riders on an out and back journey filled with hills that provide nice amounts of "airtime". The ride is actually not named after its blue paint color, but rather after the local area high schools' sports teams (when the ride opened it was the color of natural wood and was painted blue later). The ride follows an "out and back" design in which the ride goes over a series of hills before turning 180 degrees and heads back while traveling over more hills on the return to the station. There is plenty of airtime during the ride - you spend just as much time floating out of your seat as you do in it! It may not be the biggest or fastest ride at the park, but on the fun scale it ranks very high!

Ride Data
Year built: 1964
Height: 78 ft.
Top Speed: 40 mph
Designer: John Allen

In the early 90s, the park retrofitted the ride bringing it up-to-date. The update included redesigning the station, automatic brakes (many may remember back when the operator pushed or pulled a large lever to stop the train) and adding individual lap bars and head rests. Given the ride's age, Blue Streak is still in really good shape and is one of the smoother wooden roller coasters around.

Verdict: A classic ride that still runs in quite good shape for its age. With it being one of only two wooden roller coasters at the park, the experience is a unique one, not found on the many other steel coasters - a must ride!

Cadillac Cars

Type of ride: Self-driven old fashioned cars
Height Requirement: None to ride, Min. 48in to ride alone
Intensity Rating: 1/5

Family

The Cadillac Cars resemble... well, you guessed it - old Cadillac cars. Opened in the 60's and located in the front of the park, these cars are one of the more popular rides at Cedar Point.

Verdict: An classic amusement park ride; while a fun ride, it is nothing unique - ride if time permits (unless you are a family - then it is a must ride! Kids love to think they can drive!).

Calypso

Type of ride: A classic 'spin-n-puke' carinval ride
Height Requirement: Min. 46in
Intensity Rating: 3/5

If spinning around is what you fancy, Calypso is for you. Riders sit in cars that spin around inside a spin (the whole ride is spinning too). Those who have been traveling to the park for many years may remember Calypso closer to the main section of the midway before Raptor was built.

Verdict: If you like spinning, Calypso is for you. If not, stay far, far away from Calypso.

Cedar Point & Lake Erie Railroad

Type of ride: Classic amusement park train
Height Requirement: None, Min. 46in to ride alone
Intensity Rating: 1/5

The Cedar Point and Lake Erie Railroad transports guests from the Main Midway to Frontier Town. Constructed in 1963, the C.P. and L.E. RR operates many antique steam engines, each with their own name. The train loops around the back portion of the park and is a great way to go back and forth between Frontier Town and the Main Midway - especially if you aren't intrested in the shops along the Frontier Trail. The highlights of the railroad ride include passing right by Millennium Force's first drop, and Boneville, a humorous "city" of skeletons. Once on the train riders can remain on for as long as they wish.

> **Did you know...**
> The engine "Judy K" was built in 1922 and orginally was believed to have been used in mining

Train enthusiasts will appreciate the steam engines. The park has its own on site repair shop that over the years has bought steam engines from around the world and repaired them for operation on the C.P. & L.E. Railroad. While in general the park only runs one or two trains, they have several on hand that are in repair or aren't suited for use at the moment. One engine is on display along the Frontier Trail. Most recently the park traded engines with Disneyland. The engine from Disneyland is currently in the process of being rebuilt to fit the systems the C.P. & L.E. Railroad use.

Verdict: The train is not only a great way to relax, but also to transport yourself around the park - a must ride

Demon Drop

Type of ride: Freefall tower ride
Height Requirement: Min. 48in
Intensity Rating: 4/5

One of the best freefall experiences around can be found on Demon Drop. Looming 13 stories above the midway, riders are pulled up to the top of the tower, sit at the top for a second, drop and land on their back.

While the ride at first glance may look similar to Power Tower, both rides offer different experiences – the key difference being Demon Drop relies on gravity to pull the car down, while Power Tower pushes the car down using compressed air.

In 2005 it was announced that the park put Demon Drop up for sale. As this book goes to press the ride is still not sold, and according to the park will still run if not sold.

Verdict: A unique freefall experience but is rough at times - ride if time permits

Dodgem

Type of ride: Bumper cars
Height Requirement: None to ride, Min. 48in to ride alone
Intensity Rating: 3/5

✓
Family

Classic amusement park bumper cars! For the past several years the ride shuts down in early Sept as it is transformed into a "fun house" for the park's HalloWeekend's event.

Verdict: Is a trip to an amusement park complete without a ride on the bumper cars? Nope - a must ride!

Iron Dragon

Type of ride: Suspended roller coaster
Height Requirement: Min. 46in
Intensity Rating: 3/5

Iron Dragon is perhaps Cedar Point's most unique coaster. Riders sit in cars that are suspended below the track. The cars swing back and forth during the two minute and forty second ride. Iron Dragon takes riders up 72 feet and reaches speeds up to 46 miles per hour. The ride takes place over the lagoon area and twists in and out of the woods.

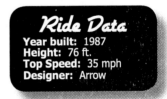

Ride Data
Year built: 1987
Height: 76 ft.
Top Speed: 35 mph
Designer: Arrow

The ride always seems to get overlooked by the brave thrill seekers and is often written off by many families as being too big for a family ride. It is a great in between ride, especially since its mininum height requirement of 46 inches is higher than the kiddy rides, but lower than most of the bigger roller coasters. We recommend taking nervous young coaster riders on Cedar

Creek Mine Ride! That is if they are tall enough to ride it (for Mine Ride one must be 48 inches tall) as thats a better "training" coaster. The straight down first drop on Iron Dragon may scare those young ones!

Verdict: Iron Dragon is very different than any other ride in the park, ride if time permits.

Matterhorn

Type of ride: Classic 'spin-n-puke' carnival ride
Height Requirement: Min. 46in
Intensity Rating: 3/5

Similar to a ride found at many carnivals, Matterhorn features cars that spin around in a circle and as the spinning increases the cars start to tilt outwards.

Verdict: If you like spinning - ride if time permits; if you don't fancy spinning stay away from the Matterhorn.

Midway Carousel

Type of ride: Carousel
Height Requirement: None, Min. 48in to ride alone
Intensity Rating: 1/5

The Midway Carousel, the oldest operating ride in the park, is a unique hand carved carousel that dates back to the early '40s. It was built in 1912 by the famous carousel carver Daniel Muller for Revere Beach Park in Massachusetts. It was moved to Cedar Point in 1946 where it was operated by a local family until the park bought the ride in 1963.

The ride features sixty hand craved horses. Amongst the horses there are four chariot-style benches in which people may ride.

Verdict: If you have an interest in merry-go-rounds/carousels then be sure to ride the Midway Carousel - it is part of a dying breed of classic carousels.

Raptor

Type of ride: Inverted roller coaster
Height Requirement: Min. 54in.
Intensity Rating: 5/5

A+

Constructed for the 1994 season, Raptor, a unique inverted style roller coaster, twists and turns its prey upside-down six times (the most on any coaster at the park). Riders sit in chairs (think ski lift style) that hang below the track, allowing riders' feet to dangle freely.

Riders become bird-like through the two minute plus adventure that is Raptor. One minute you're right side up. The next you are being twisted and turned upside down twice within a matter of seconds in the "cobra roll." Then you are kicking the sky in the huge vertical loop. When most rides start to let up, Raptor takes its prey through a double helix at the end of the ride providing some of the most intense positive G-forces found on any other roller coaster.

Ride Data
Year built: 1994
Height: 137 ft.
Top Speed: 57 mph
Designer: B&M

Raptor, one of the more popular rides to this day, can be argued to be the park's biggest success story. It was in 1994 the park reached a new season high attendance record. There is a reason behind it - Raptor always ranks high in polls of the best roller coasters in the world.

Verdict: If fast, intense roller coasters are for you, then Raptor is an must ride. It will become an experience you won't soon forget.

Raptor flies through the vertical loop

Scrambler

Type of ride: Classic 'spin-n-puke' carnival ride
Height Requirement: Min. 48in
Intensity Rating: 3/5

The Scrambler is just like a giant egg scrambler. Riders sit in cars that spin in a circle at high speeds.

Verdict: If you like spinning - ride if time permits; if you don't fancy spinning stay away!

Sky Ride

Type of ride: Cable cars
Height Requirement: None, Min. 48in to ride alone
Intensity Rating: 1/5

The Sky Ride is a great way to travel up and down the Main Midway, with stations located at either end. Lines for the Sky Ride are long at the start of the day to travel from the entrance toward Iron Dragon and vice versa as the day wraps up. For minimal waits, ride Sky Ride toward the front of the park, in the morning, vice versa at night. It is a one-way ride, you must re-enter.

✓
Family

Verdict: A nice, classic amusement park attraction - ride if time permits if you don't mind heights.

Turnpike Cars

Type of ride: Mini "hot rods" which anyone can drive
Height Requirement: None, Min. 48in to ride alone
Intensity Rating: 1/5

The Turnpike Cars are mini hot rods from the 50's.

Verdict: A fun little ride for the kids, nothing more than just that

Wildcat

Type of ride: Wild mouse style roller coaster
Height Requirement: Min. 48in
Intensity Rating: 4/5

It may be small, but it sure packs a wild punch. Wildcat takes riders through hairpin turns and numerous drops on its small, but tightly packed together course.

Ride Data
Year built: 1970
Height: 50 ft.
Track Length: 1,837 ft.
Designer: Schwarzkopf

   Verdict: While the ride may look small, it is
in fact one of the more intense roller coasters
in the park due to its constant (and sometimes
rough) sharp turns and countless drops. If you
don't mind a intense roller coaster then Wildcat is a must ride.

Entertainment

          The Main Midway offers entertainment for everyone and is home
to the biggest productions in the park. Just inside the Cedar Point gates is the
Centennial Theatre which offers musicial style shows during the summer and
a magic show during HalloWeekends. While the theatre is small is size, the
productions are always crowd favorites and are known to win awards. The
two other shows found on the Main Midway are so big they deserve their own
breakdown:

Snoopy Rocks! On Ice

          Those who have visited the park in the past may remember a
large theatre near the middle of the park that used to show IMAX movies.
The theatre is still there, but the screen has been replaced with an ice rink
and instead of IMAX movies Snoopy and his gang put on a live-action ice
show. The show, which lasts around a half hour is a fun filled musicial-style
production about the lives of the different Peanut gang characters. Joining the
characters is a cast of highly skilled ice dancers that skate and jump
and provide an incredibly unique element to the show. Be sure to
arrive early as not only does the show usually fill up on busy days,
but the pre-show is not to be missed. The characters are known to
stop by the pre-show! The performance runs from Mid-June through
mid-August.

Hot Summer Lights

          Each night from early June through August (check with park for
exact dates if you are visiting in later August, as sometime it is only shown
on the weekends at that point) at 10pm the Main Midway (near Iron Dragon)
comes to life! Hot Summer Lights is a nighttime spectacular featuring fireworks, lasers, and music all wrapped up to create an enjoyable experience.
Take note that the rides around the area close down before the preformance
due to the fireworks and other effects involved. If you don't plan on watching

the show or plan to spend another evening at the park to watch the show - it is a GREAT time to ride other rides. Once the show starts many of the rides near the back of the park begin to empty out, which means shorter lines for you!

Food

The Main Midway offers the most diverse collection of places to get food in the park. Below is a list of the main establishments along with some of the favorite food stands/outlets.

* **Burger Patio** - located near Raptor, counter-service, serves burgers and chicken fingers.
* **Coasters** - located at the tip of the Main Midway near Iron Dragon, 50's theme, counter-service, serves burgers, chicken filets, onion rings shakes, malts, and even root beer floats.
* **Corral** - located near Raptor and Cedar Downs, serves funnel cakes, corn dogs, pizza, and other snack items.
* **Donut Time** - located near the front of the park. Donut Time actu ally opens before the park (guests are allowed to enter the park up to Donut Time) and provides donuts, cookies, cinammon rolls, breads, muffins and Starbucks coffee. Internet access is also available. Kids will love being able to watch the donuts being made! Donut Time is the perfect place to grab breakfast when arriving in the morn ing and is a great place to grab some snacks (and coffee!) for the ride home.
* **Game Day Grille** - full-service restaurant offering burgers, wings, pork sandwhiches and plenty of TVs to catch your favorite sporting event.
* **Hot Potato** - located under Raptor's first drop, Hot Potato serves up delicious large french fries that can be topped off with chilli and/or cheese.
* **Hurricane Hannah's** - new for the 2006 season and located liter ally right inside the park's main gate, Hurrican Hannah's is a tropical themed counter-service food station that serves food with a Caribbean twist - speciality pizza, Cuban Panini, Calypso Chicken Wrap and more. The location is one of the only non-restaurant establishments in the park in which beer is served.

- **Ice Cream Parlour** - located across the midway from Raptor, serves hand-dipped ice cream, milk shakes and taffy
- **Johnny Rockets** - full service restaurant located across the midway from Raptor's first drop. 50's style chain-restruant that serves up your favorite grille food from chicken fingers to burgers. Their famous chili and fries are available - just ask your waiter or waitress who can be found singing and dancing to the classic hits of that day and age. Johnny Rocket's is especially known for their flavored sodas and made-to-order shakes.
- **Midway Market** - full service, pay-one-price buffet restruant located near the entrance to Raptor. The buffet features popular American, Italian and international dishes along with a just for kids section and a dessert bar. Lunch is offered from 11-3, while dinner is served from 3-close. Yes, the buffet can **$$$** be pricey (exact prices not available at press time) but chances are if you visit the buffet for lunch, you won't need to eat much else throughout the day. As much money as the buffet may seem, remember you are in an amusement park. Elsewhere throughout the park you will be paying nearly three dollars for a twenty ounce bottle of pop, so it is all pricey!

Games

No amusement park would be complete without an arcade. The Main Midway is home to not one, but several aracades. The biggest one, which features DDR machines is located in the lower level of the coliseum ballroom. Arcades throughout the midway feature plenty of the classic amusement park game - skeeball. Good luck!

Shops

The Main Midway offers a wide range of shops. Park Plaza is one of the largest shops in the park and is located right inside the park's main gates. It features everything Cedar Point and chances are if the other stores don't have it, Park Plaza will. Snoopy Boutique offers not only everything Snoopy and the Peanuts gang related but also offers an whole collection of candy! The Pagonda Gift Shop offers Cedar Point related merchandise along with a variety of completely random souvenir style gifts (a large collection of candy located near the back of the store! Hatitudes is Cedar Point's version of a "goth store" selling shirts and gifts geared toward teenagers and adults.

6

Wicked Twister Midway

The Wicked Twister Midway has some of the park's craziest rides, yet is also home to some of the mildest rides. Located on the east side of the park – the midway runs from the convention area to the south end (Disaster Transport).

Highlights include the Cedar Point's version of the ferris wheel - The Giant Wheel, and the twisted steel creation of a roller coaster - Wicked Twister.

Chaos

Type of ride: Classic 'spin-n-puke' carnival ride
Height Requirement: Min. 48in
Intensity Rating: 5/5

Chaos is just what the name says, chaos! Riders sit in a vechicle that spins every which way. Just looking at this would even make our friends who don't like spinning dizzy!

Verdict: If you like spinning, and by spinning I mean spinning in complete chaos (pardon the pun) - ride if time permits.

Diaster Transport

Type of ride: Indoor roller coaster
Height Requirement: Min. 46in
Intensity Rating: 3/5

Disaster Transport was originally built in 1985 as Avalanche Run. In 1990 Cedar Point enclosed the ride and added an outer space theme with many special effects. Disaster Transport is an indoor bobsled coaster where riders board a shuttle (roller coaster car) and begin a journey to Alaska. Along the way a disaster occurs and the shuttle starts to go out of control. Do you make it to Alaska? You'll just have to ride to find out!

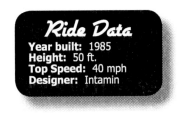

Ride Data
Year built: 1985
Height: 50 ft.
Top Speed: 40 mph
Designer: Intamin

Verdict: While the ride is unqiue in the sense that its indoors, the ride itself is nothing special and should only be ridden if time permits (or if its really hot outside - the queue is air conditioned!). To be fair, it is a great ride for the entire family. In that case, for families - it is a must ride.

Giant Wheel

Type of ride: Ferris wheel
Height Requirement: None, Min. 48in to ride alone
Intensity Rating: 5/5

A+ ✓ Family

The Giant Wheel is Cedar Point's ferris wheel (what's an amusement park without one?). The views from the Giant Wheel are simply spectacular. Located along the beach, the wheel offers a view of Lake Erie on one side and the park on the other.

Verdict: Classic amusement park ride - a must ride.

maXair

Type of ride: Frisbee spinning ride
Height Requirement: Min. 52in.
Intensity Rating: 5/5

maXair is easily one of the most intimating rides ever created. Riders sit on the outside of a giant circle that rotates while swing like a giant pendulum. Oh, and their feet dangle freely in the wind. The ride begins simply enough - slowly spinning in a circle, but as it picks up speed, so does the ride. It starts to swing back and forth, and while it does not swing completly around, depending on the rotation of the seats many riders may be upside at times!). After spinning back and forth while swinging back and forth several times the ride slows down and brings riders back to a "sense of normal."

Verdict: It is one of the more intense rides in the park, but also one of the best. If spinning is you thing - a must ride.r

maXair spins out of control both above and below

Ocean Motion

Type of ride: Pirate ship ride
Height Requirement: None
Intensity Rating: 3/5

Argh there matey! Ocean Motion is a giant pirate ship that swings back and forth just like the ships on the high seas!

Verdict: While a fun ride, only ride if you have had a chance to experience everything else. The ride is one found at most parks and carnivals

Space Spiral

Type of ride: Observayion tower
Height Requirement: None, Min. 46in. to ride alon
Intensity Rating: 0/5

Space Spiral is one of the tallest, yet perhaps the least intense ride in the park. Riders sit in a enclosed cabin that slowly rotates up a large tower, providing some stunning views of the park.

Verdict: The ride provides those who may be too nervous to ride the other tall rides a chance to see the park from up high. While nothing special, the views on the ride justify riding if time permits (but it is a GREAT family ride!).

Troika

Type of ride: Classic spin-n-puke ride
Height Requirement: Min. 48in.
Intensity Rating: 3/5

A classic carnival-style spining ride.

Verdict: While a fun ride, only ride if you have had a chance to experience everything else, since the ride is one found at most parks and carnivals.

Wicked Twister

Type of ride: Launched impluse roller coaster
Height Requirement: Min. 52in.
Intensity Rating: 5/5

A+

Wicked Twister, an impulse coaster built in 2002, gives a whole new meaning to the word "twisted". Riders board inverted cars in which their feet dangle freely. With a brief countdown, the train fires from 0-50 in 2 seconds flat! The car flies down

Ride Data
Year built: 2002
Height: 215 ft.
Top Speed: 72 mph
Designer: Intamin

the track, turns straight up and twists up the forward tower. Next it travels in reverse, right through the station – and up the back tower. Twist and repeat.

Verdict: While it may not look or be considered by some to be a "traditional" roller coaster, Wicked Twister is one of the top roller coasters at Cedar Point. Its unique elements - launching, fast speed, going backwards, oh and twisting up to 450 degrees, makes it a must ride - that is if you don't mind being twisted!

Entertainment

The Wicked Twister Midway offers one show - the diving show. It takes place in the former dolphin "stadium", and features performers diving from all kinds of heights in the high-energy, entertaining show. While the show may not sound like much it is always very fun.

Food

The Wicked Twister Midway is home to one sit-down restaurant and several counter-service locations. Located near Peanuts Playground, Macaroni's, a full-service restaurant, serves up pizza, pasta, and other Italian dishes. The food always seems to be top-notch. The location is "off-the-beaten-path" so to speak, therefore providing a relaxing atmosphere (there are no high energy rides rocketing by every minute). Across from the aquatic stadium is Mr. Potato - one of the three locations in the park to purchase the famous Cedar Point french fries.

Games

One of the area's unqiue features is the gaming plaza. Filled with numerous classic "carnival" style games, the plaza has an art deco feel that is a throw back to the old-style amusement parks of the 50's and 60's.

7

Frontier Trail / Town

The Frontier Trail/Town is perhaps the most beautiful and unique part of Cedar Point. It is a wooden area themed loosely on the frontier. The Frontier Trail begins at the plaza in front of Millennium Force. Heading down the trail there are numerous shops selling unique gifts such as a glassblowing shop, a candle shop – where you can make your own candles, and a woodworking shop. There is just something to be said for walking down a heavily wooded path with unique shops selling your favorite amusement park snacks (fudge, funnel cakes, and large cookies) and seeing someone hand carve something out of wood, all the while smelling the barbeque chicken from the Grist Mill.

Frontier Town offers many shops, restaurants, and rides with a frontier theme. In the center of Frontier Town there are the Antique Cars and a small town plaza. There is even a museum. Walking down that path you will find the Chuck Wagon Inn, Last Chance Saloon, Lusty Lil's Palace, and at the very end of the path, Mean Streak and the Frontier Town Station for the Cedar Point and Lake Erie Railroad.

Highlights of the Frontier Trail include Millennium Force, the candle shop, and Grist Mill refreshments, where on a summer day the smell of the BBQ chicken seems to take over the area!

Rides

Antique Cars

Type of ride: Mini drive-them-yourself-cars
Height Requirement: None, Min. 48in. to ride alone
Intensity Rating: 1/5

The Antique Cars are little old fashioned cars that can be driven aorund a set path. The car's path goes through many turns and even over a covered bridge.

Did You Know...
The Antique Cars along with both the Turnpike & Cadillac Cars run gasohol to help the environment

Verdict: A fun little ride for the kids (or those young at heart!), nothing more than just that - though the ride always seems to be a hit amongst all families.

Cedar Creek Mine Ride

Type of ride: Runaway mine train roller coaster
Height Requirement: Min. 48in.
Intensity Rating: 3/5

A+ ✓ Family

Cedar Creek Mine Ride, or better known as Mine Ride, is a small runaway mine train roller coaster that is loosely themed to around a mine! The ride begins by going up the 48 ft. lift but before going down any drops the ride cruises through a few turns then gently drops over the water before entering a helix and climbing a second lift. The

Ride Data
Year built: 1969
Height: 48 ft.
Ride Time: 2.5 mins
Designer: Arrow

second part of the ride is a series of helixes. While the ride isn't as fast or as tall as the park's other roller coasters, the Mine Ride ranks high on the fun scale.

Verdict: While the ride is perfect for a family, it is very enjoyable no matter what your age - a must ride

Cedar Point & Lake Erie Railroad

One of two stations is located in Frontier Town near Mean Streak. For more information on the train please see page 32.

Mantis

Type of ride: Stand-up roller coaster
Height Requirement: Min. 54in.
Intensity Rating: 5/5

Unlike all the other roller coasters at Cedar Point, you stand up for this once in a lifetime experience. Mantis riders stand in a car over bicycle-like seats. This is one mean bug! It will take you up 145 feet, drop you at a 52-degree angle, and spin you through 4 inversions. Can you stand it?

Ride Data
Year built: 1996
Height: 145 ft.
Top Speed: 60 mph
Designer: B&M

Verdict: A very unique and enjoyable ride, but be warned, it is one of the most intense rides in the park. If you can "stand" the intensity (pardon the pun) then it is a must ride.

Maverick

Type of ride: Launched runaway mine ride roller coaster
Height Requirement: Min. 48in.
Intensity Rating: 5/5

The old west was never this wild! New-for-2007, Maverick is a high-tech roller coaster experience that plans to give its riders a taste of an out of control horse chase! At the time of printing, the ride has yet to open, but it sure looks promising.

Ride Data
Year built: 2007
Height: 105 ft.
Top Speed: 70 mph
Designer: Intamin

The runaway mine themed train begins the ride by climbing a 105 ft. tall hill before plummeting down at a 95 degree angle - thats right, the drop is below 90 degrees (one of the few rides in the world to do such a thing). Following the drop the train remains relativiely close to the ground as it flys past a all types of mine themeing and goes through two corkscrews and then over a small hill. Think its over? Not quite! The ride then launchs through an enclosed, pitch black tunnel before flying out and traveling over a mid-size hill before swooping back down and into a ground-hugging heartline spin inversion. Over a few more small hills and Maverick races into the station.

Verdict: Not available at publishing deadline

Maverick under construction in late 2006

Mean Streak

Type of ride: Wooden twister roller coaster
Height Requirement: Min. 48in.
Intensity Rating: 4/5

The name may call it mean but the ride itself looks far from it. Its large structure makes it look spectacular and graceful from the ground despite the ride being a different story. Expecting a "smooth as glass" ride from this wooden roller coaster is a far fetched idea.

Ride Data
Year built: 1991
Height: 161 ft.
Top Speed: 65 mph
Designer: Summers

When it opened in 1991, Mean Streak was the tallest and fastest roller coaster in the world. The ride twists and turns around itself several times and races over hill after hill. The layout, especially for those who haven't ridden many times, confuses riders and makes them wonder where they are headed next. ITis constantly turning and twisting and going under its own self.

Verdict: A fun ride, if you don't mind wooden roller coasters, and if you don't mind some roughness - ride if time permits!

Millennium Force

Type of ride: Giga roller coaster
Height Requirement: Min. 48in.
Intensity Rating: 4/5

A+

Cedar Point was the first park to break the 200 feet height mark on a roller coaster, and in 2000 decided to break the 300 ft threshold with Millennium Force. Standing 310 feet off the ground, this ride is like no other. Its top speed may be 93mph, but unlike any other coaster, it maintains a fast pace the entire way through. At the end of the ride it is still going over 50 mph!

Ride Data
Year built: 2000
Height: 310 ft.
Top Speed: 93 mph
Designer: Intamin

Those brave enough to ride the "Force" will notice one thing fast - there isn't much to hold them - just a simple seat belt and T style lapbar that comes up between their legs and rests around their wasit. The cars themself are practically sideless and feature slight stadium style seating - creating a very open environment (which is not something the mind likes if you are nervous!). Nothing can prepare riders for the moment when the ride begins and the cars gets yanked quickly out of the station and up the hill.

Unlike most other roller coasters, Millennium Force features a unique elevator style lift system instead of the normal chain. The lift is fast (less than 25 seconds to get to the top) and is near silent - the perfect chance to ponder how crazy you were to get on the ride. But before you can come up with an answer, the train crests the hill and begins to plummet. The feeling you get as you are pulled over and down the 310 foot hill is like none other. Before you realize it you experienced one of the biggest roller coaster drops in the world. The train goes full speed up into the first turnaround at such a angle you feel as if you are nearly upside down. The train then rockets down and around into a tunnel - you're going so fast that if you blink you wouldn't know there was a tunnel - and then up the ride's third hill. This would be a good time to mention that Millennium Force's third hill, key word THIRD, is taller than 13 out of the 16 other roller coasters in the park. The train gracefully flys over the third hill giving the riders the extreme sensation of floating. The train then goes through two tightly, near inverted turns, before going over a fourth hill that again provides the sensation of floating like never before. The train, which seems to be running on steroids, plunges into another tunnel. Be sure to try to smile - they take your picture in the tunnel which is perfect since most of your friends probably won't believe that you actually rode it. After the tunnel, the ride rushes over another hill and then twists up over the queue into the final turn before cruising, cruising (as in still going over 50mph), into the final brakes

Millennium Force is simply like no other ride - its very graceful. The ride is so smooth you'll feel like you are floating. Its so fast you feel like you are part of the Indy 500. Oh yes, its tall too - tall enough a good eye can spot it over ten miles away.

Verdict: Without a doubt Millennium Force is a must ride. Wait in line if you have to, run to the ride early in the morning to beat the crowds - its all worth it. Look up adreline rush or roller coaster in the dictionary and their defintions should be two words: Millennium Force.

Skyhawk

Type of ride: Giant swinging style ride
Height Requirement: Min. 48in.
Intensity Rating: 4/5

Remember when you were a little kid and were trying to swing over the top of the swing-set, let alone past horizontal, but it never happened? Problem solved! Skyhawk is one giant swing that gives riders the experience of going farther, higher, and faster than they have ever gone before on a swing.

Plain and simple - its a really fun ride. Without much warning the ride takes off and the speed just keeps building up with each swing. Using a compressed air system similar to Power Tower, the ride pushes and pulls riders back and forth while their feet dangle freely. As the ride swings up to its highest point (which is not completely upside down but rather about 75%), instead of gravity pulling it back to earth the ride is pushed back down (faster than gravity). Depending on which side of the ride you sit, you'll get a different experience and unique views (that is if you are brave enough to look around while up in the air!)

Verdict: It provides a thrill but doesn't make you want to lose the elephant ear you just had. It will, however, bring the kid out of you! A really fun ride - a must ride!

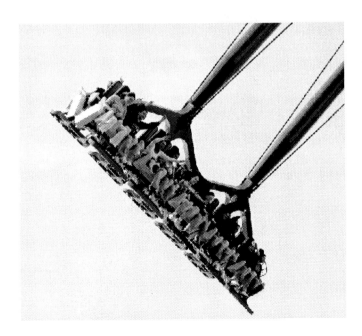

Snake River Falls

Type of ride: Flume water ride
Height Requirement: Min. 48in.
Intensity Rating: 3/5

If you like water, and like to get VERY WET, Snake River Falls is for you. You are guaranteed to get completely soaked. The ride starts by climbing up the 82-foot high lift. When the boat crests the top of the lift, it starts to slowly float in water. It goes around a 180-degree turn before the drop. The boat rushes down the flume and hits the water causing a powerful wall of water. Near the bottom of the drop there is a bridge (which rides use to exit the ride) that goes over the boats path and thus making it a big target for the wall of water. If you didn't get wet enough or want to get wetter, be sure to stand on the bridge after the ride! It is quite an experience being hit with a wall of water.

Verdict: Like water? If so, then Snake River Falls is for you! Ride if time permits. You'll probably need to change clothes since when you ride Snake River Falls you'll get wet but is a fun experience.

Thunder Canyon

Type of ride: Water ride
Height Requirement: Min. 46in.
Intensity Rating: 2/5

Thunder Canyon is a white water river adventure. Soon-to-be-soaked riders board a 12 person circular raft. Thunder Canyon takes riders through rapids and under waterfalls. The ride takes many by surprise because of the ending, most of the ride is not visible from the midway.

Verdict: See Snake River Fall's verdict above!

Wave Swinger

Type of ride: Swing style carnival ride
Height Requirement: Min. 48in.
Intensity Rating: 2/5

On Wave Swinger, riders sit in small swings that spin around and around in circles.

Verdict: Ride if time permits since you can find this ride at nearly every park and carnival

Misc. Attraction

Town Hall Museum

One of the most unique attractions at Cedar Point is the Town Hall Museum. Located near Skyhawk, Town Hall features an extensive collection of items from Cedar Point's past. As you read in the history chapter Cedar Point is the second oldest park therefore it has a long and rich history. The Town Hall Museum features everything from old postcards and arcade games to different signs and banners from special events. The Museum is also how to the numerous world record plaques and various awards the park has won over the years.

Petting Farm

The Frontier Trail is home to a unique attraction - a petting farm. The farm, which surrounds a big red barn, features farm animals which guests can interact with and even feed.

Food

The Frontier Trail/Town is home to the diverse collection of food options in the park. There are the usual fast-service stands, two saloon style theatres that sells snacks and drinks, and a cafeteria style restaurant.

Red Garter Saloon combines both live entertainment and food and drinks to create a fun spot to grab a quick bite or drink. It offers some of the best entertainment in the park. Each year bring s a new show schedule with it. During the summer months there are two different shows that play on the same day. Beer and wine coolers are available, and on the food end there are small snacks and meals. Similar to the Red Garter Saloon, Palace Theatre has live entertainment and offers food and drink . The theatre is only open during the shows.

Did You Know...

On average over 120 unqiue costumes are used for each seperate live show at the park

Between shows guests can get drinks and snacks at the neighboring Last Chance Saloon. The Chuck Wagon Inn offers chicken and other southern cooking items in a cafeteria style format. The Frontier Inn is a counter-service food outlet offering pizza, pasta, breadsticks (which are really good!) and salad.

One highlight of the array of fast-service stands is Grist Mill Refreshments. Throughout the year, usually from the afternoon onward, chicken is barbequed outside. The smell alone is great and the food lives up to the smell (not to mention it is a nice break from the usual amusement park food).

Shops

Unlike the shops in the park or in any park the shops along the Frontier Trail are a key component of the trail section of the midway and are quite special. Along the trail there are over a dozen small shops that offer specalized gifts that are unique (read: not cheesy amusement park gifts). The various shops are housed in small log-cabin like structures that line the wooden path giving the area a rustic, relaxing feel. The following page offers a brief description of each.

- **Berry Market** - A shop specializing in canned berries featuring the famous Knott's Berry Farms jams.
- **Blacksmith** - Small shop that offers blacksmith demonstrations
- **Candle Shop** - This unique store that sells all different kinds of candles but the main attraction is the fact guests can purchase small candles which they can then dip into hot wax to color the candle. (The candles make a great souvenir!).
- **Candy Shop** - A shop that sells all kinds of tasty treats.
- **China Shop** - A small shop that sells a large number of china plates
- **Frontier Merchant** - Sells different western and Cedar Point themed gifts.
- **Glass Shop** - A shop that sells various items made out of glass. In the back of the store is a small theatre where glass blowing demonstra tions takes place throughout the day.
- **Leather Shop** - Located in a mock up of "Fort Sandusky" the leather shop sells wallets, belts and other items crafted out of leather.
- **Olde Time Photo Shop** - A photograpthy studio where guests, for a price, can dress up in old western clothing and get their picture taken with an old western backdrop or theme.
- **Pottery Shop** - A shop that sells various pottery goods
- **Signmaker** - A small stand that makes custom signs out of wood
- **Teddy Bear Company** - A shop that lets guests make their own teddy bear.
- **Woodworking** - A shop which sells unique items, of all sizes, carved out of wood. At various times a craftsman is on hand demonstrating the art of wood carving.

Entertainment

The Frontier Trail/Town has plenty to offer when it comes to entertainment. Both the Red Garter Saloon and the Palace Theatre offer small-scale, music-based productions which generally run just under a half hour. The shows usually have some musical theme and feature numerous singers, dancers, and musicians playing songs that fit within the show's theme.

Show times are posted near both theatres or can be found in the show guide brochure supplement that is available throughout the park.

8

Top Thrill Dragster Midway

The Top Thrill Dragster Midway begins where the Corkscrew roller coaster crosses over the midway (near Power Tower) and extends north to the railroad track crossing near Gemini. The midway, which very well could be nicknamed the "midway of the giants" (3 out of the 4 roller coasters were once the tallest in the world), is home to everything from the world's tallest roller coaster – to Cedar Point's smallest coaster. Not-to-mention, the younger ones will find two "kiddy areas" – Camp Snoopy and the Jr. Gemini Kids Area (for more information on the kiddy rides, see the chapter titled "Kiddy Areas").

Corkscrew

Type of ride: Looping roller coaster
Height Requirement: Min. 48in.
Intensity Rating: 3/5

Built in 1976, Corkscrew was the very first coaster to turn riders upside down three times. At 85 ft high, Corkscrew may not be the biggest or fastest, but it is a fun ride.

Ride Data
Year built: 1976
Height: 85 ft.
Top Speed: 48 mph
Designer: Arrow

Verdict: While the ride is fun, it is showing its age and can be quite rough at times - ride if time permits.

Gemini

Type of ride: Racing roller coaster
Height Requirement: Min. 48in.
Intensity Rating: 3/5

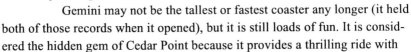

Gemini may not be the tallest or fastest coaster any longer (it held both of those records when it opened), but it is still loads of fun. It is considered the hidden gem of Cedar Point because it provides a thrilling ride with a lot of airtime, head choppers, and speed. True to its name, the Gemini features twin trains that race along the course. Be sure to sit on the inside part of the car (that is the side closest to the other side of the ride) and at times you just may be able to slap hands with the other train!

Ride Data
Year built: 1978
Height: 125 ft.
Top Speed: 60 mph
Designer: Arrow

Verdict: Sometimes bigger doesn't mean better and Gemini proves it - a must ride!

Magnum XL-200

Type of ride: Hyper roller coaster
Height Requirement: Min. 48in.
Intensity Rating: 4/5

A+

In 1989, Cedar Point decided to take roller coasters to a new limit with Magnum XL-200. At 205 feet tall, it was the first roller coaster to break the 200-foot barrier.

Magnum begins with the long climb to the top of the 205 foot hill – the climb alone is one minute! Many people, including this author, found Magnum more scary than Millennium Force and other taller roller coasters because it takes so long to get to the top – so much time to rethink your decision to ride (so if you don't like heights this really isn't the ride for you!). Following the first drop the ride begins to travel along the park's beach area. If you are brave enough to look around, Magnum offers what usually is agreed upon as the greatest view from a roller coaster (some even argue on a clear

Ride Data
Year built: 1989
Height: 205 ft.
Top Speed: 72 mph
Designer: Arrow

day Canada is visible!). After a second and third hill, the ride rages through a large pretzel shaped turnaround and begins a long series of small hills, dubbed "bunny hills", on its return trip. While the hills may be small, their design creates numerous "airtime" moments – the moments when your body is actually floating in air.

Verdict: It may be some 18 years old, but Magnum still ranks as one of the top roller coasters in the world in nearly every roller coaster poll, and there is a good reason for that - a must ride!

Magnum's 205 ft. first hill

Monster

Type of ride: Carnival style spin-n-puke ride
Height Requirement: Min. 48in.
Intensity Rating: 4/5

Sometimes known as the spider ride at local carnivals, the Monster is only for people who have a strong stomach. Riders board a vehicle and spin around, while the entire ride frame spins and moves up and down.

Verdict: If you like to spin, ride if time permits, since it is found at nearly every park and carnival

Paddlewheel Excursion

Type of ride: Boat tour ride
Height Requirement: None, Min. 46in to ride alone
Intensity Rating: 0/5

A+ ✓ Family

In the middle of the park is a small river called Cedar Creek and it is home to Paddlewheel Excursion. Riders embard on a ten minute journey around the river as their captain tells corny jokes and takes the boat past many entertaining spots.

Verdict: Paddle Wheel Excursions is a great way to relax, get off your feet, and smile - a must ride

Power Tower

Type of ride: Drop ride
Height Requirement: Min. 52in.
Intensity Rating: 3/5

A+

Power Tower features two Space Shot towers and two Turbo Drop towers. The Turbo Drop towers take riders up slowly, pauses for a brief few seconds (unless you're on the ride then it seems like forever) at the top, and then drops them back to earth. The Space Shot towers blasts riders straight up, then bounces them back down to earth.

Ride Data
Year built: 1998
Ride Height: 240 ft
Tower Height: 300 ft.
Designer: S&S

Verdict: Power Tower appears much more intense than it really is. Add in the fact that it is smoother than glass and fun, it's a must ride

Super Himalaya
Type of ride: Carnival style spin-n-puke ride
Height Requirement: Min. 46in.
Intensity Rating: 2/5

One of the many rides at Cedar Point that well simply spins around in a circle. It is also found at most carnivals.

Verdict: Nothing special, but fun if you enjoying spinning rides - ride if time permits

Top Thrill Dragster
Type of ride: Launched strata roller coaster
Height Requirement: Min. 48in.
Intensity Rating: 5/5

A+

Standing an astonishing 420 feet above earth, Top Thrill Dragster has been appropriately coined the world's first "strata-coaster" since from the ground it appears to enter the stratosphere! Based on a drag race, Top Thrill Dragster has been themed heavily to match its "storyline"(it even has a grand-stand area for those who prefer rides under 100 mph).

Riders board one of six, sixteen passenger trains that, after a short count-down (much like a real drag race there are lights that flash different colors as it counts down), launch from 0-120 mph in a mere 4 seconds. Before riders know it, the train yanks them straight up and travels several hundred feet before making a sharp 90-degree twist and then flies over the top. After the train

crests the hill it twists 270 degrees followed
by a vertical drop before quickly pulling out
and hitting the brakes.

Verdict: Its fast, its quick, its intense (the
launch is one of the most intense moments
of any roller coaster), but if you don't mind
traveling nearly double the legal highway speed limit then Dragster is a must
ride, after all, when else can you travel (legally) over 100mph?

Ride Data

Year built: 2003
Height: 420 ft.
Top Speed: 120 mph
Designer: Intamin

Witches Wheel

Type of ride: Carnival style spin-n-puke ride
Height Requirement: Min. 48in., Min 60in. to ride alone
Intensity Rating: 2/5

If spinning upside down is your type of ride, be sure to ride Witches
Wheel. The ride starts off slow enough, but as it picks up speed and begins to
tilt the ground and sky become a blur as riders are spun upside down too many
times to count.

Verdict: If you don't mind extreme spinning, and not knowing what side is
up, then this is a must ride!

Entertainment

While there is no "real" entertainment, as in shows or events
on the Top Thrill Dragster Midway, the area does offer entertainment seekers a special treat. Located next to Top Thrill Dragster is a set of grand stand
bleachers. Watching the faces on nervous Dragster riders just before they
launch is entertainment in itself - great entertainment at that! It is also a great
spot to take a picture of people you know who are on the ride - their facial
expresion is something you'll most likely want to capture - especially if they
never ridden Dragster before!

Food

The Top Thrill Dragster Midway is the only one in the park
that does not offer a full-service style restruant. The food selection is on the
smaller side on this midway, so if you are hungry, your best be headed else-
where! Numerous food stands can be found including the Happy Friar, which
serves up Cedar Point's famous large-style french fries. Under the Top Thrill

Dragster grandstand there are a few foot outlets offering hot dogs and other snacks. Numerous other small stand and food outlets line the midway offering your favorite theme park snacks.

Shops

Much like the selection of food, the Top Thrill Dragster Midway doesn't offer much when it comes to shops. One exception is Speed Zone, located across the midway from Top Thrill Dragster's station. Speed Zone is one of the more complete gift shops in the park and it focuses mainly on Cedar Point related items. Located near the base of Top Thrill Dragster's mighty tower is a booth where caricatures are offered.

9
Kiddy Areas

Cedar Point is known world-wide for its collection of record-breaking roller coasters. A lesser known fact is that the park offers plenty for the younger crowd. All kiddy rides (except where noted) are reserved for children under 54 inches tall.

Camp Snoopy

Added for the 1999 season, Camp Snoopy is an area themed around Snoopy and his gang. Throughout the day, Snoopy and his gang make appearances in the area.

Camp Snoopy is a perfect area for the family since it is filled with rides for not just young children but those who are in between the kid and adult rides. Red Baron lets those kids who want to be a pilot "test" their skills - they even get to control whether their plane goes up or down! On Peanuts 500 young children get to take part in a mini car race. The Camp Bus slowly takes its passengers up and down - preparing for the likes of Power Tower and Demon Drop.

The Tilt-A-Wheel is one of the few rides in the park that a family can enjoy together. Ride wise it is just like the name says, a standard tilt-a-wheel atraction just like the one most carnivals offer. Lolli Swings is a miniature version of the Wave Swinger. Balloon Race is for kids who love to spin. Kids sit in "balloons" that spin in a circle while they can control how much they rotate (parents - its always a great photo op!).

The marquee attraction in Camp Snoopy is Woodstock Express, a family roller coaster that is sure to please coaster fans of all ages. At a height of 38 feet, Woodstock Express is bigger than Jr. Gemini, yet smaller than Mine Ride or Iron Dragon. It is not only a great "training coaster" for future coaster lovers, but has the word family written all over it. Don't forget to smile for the on-ride photo camera.

| Height Restriction Chart ||
Ride Name	Restrictions
Balloon Race	Min. 42in, Max. 54in.
Camp Bus	Under 54in.
Lolli Swings	Under 54in.
Peanuts 500	Under 54in.
Tilt-A-Wheel	None, Min. 46in. to ride alone
Woodstrock Express	Min. 36in.

Jr. Gemini Kids Area

Located around Jr Gemini, the Jr. Gemini Kids Area is a cluster of rides mainly geared toward the younger kids (those under 54in.). The area is home to several small rides in which kids can ride around in circles in different kinds of cars. The "Kiddy Bumper Boats" allow kids to float around (slowly) in little bumper boats - but no one gets wet on this one! Frog Hopper is a mini version of Power Tower - allowing kids to get a slow, short feel of the real thing! The namesake of the area - Jr. Gemini (see ride data at right) is a small roller coaster. At a height of 19 feet and a top speed of 6 mph, Jr. Gemini offers those not-quite-tall-enough-to-ride-the-real-thing crowd a chance to find out what a roller coaster really is.

Ride Data
Year built: 1979
Height: 19 ft.
Top Speed: 6 mph
Designer: Intamin

Height Restriction Chart	
Ride Name	Restrictions
Frog Hopper	Between 36in. and 54in.
Jr. Gemini	Under 54in. (though a parent may ride a child)
Kiddy Bumper Boats	Between 36in. and 54in.

Kiddy Kingdom

Kiddy Kingdom is a kingdom of kiddy rides. The area is home to some of the more "average" rides – likes those you would find at your local carnival among other rides. One highlight among them is a children's version of the famous old amusement park attraction the roto-whip. It was a staple in nearly every amusement park back in the day. The signature ride is the Kiddy Carousel (which anyone may ride) that features not just horses, but all kinds of animals.

Did you know... One of the horses on the carousel in Kiddy Kingdom was featured on an USPS postal stamp

Krazy Kars is a kid version of bumper cars. Sir-Rub-A-Dub's Tub is a small water ride in which kids float around in small tubes (no one gets wet, but parents may ride with the children). Sky Fighters lets kids become pilots as they get to control the up and down movement of their own plane as it spins in a circle. 4x4s allows the younger children to drive their very own (and even their own size) monster truck.

All of the rides, unless otherwise noted, are reserved for those under 54in.

Peanuts Playground

All of the rides, unless otherwise noted, are reserved for those under 54in. Peanuts Playground features swings, slides, etc. In the middle of the playground is a mini- amphitheater. Peanuts Express is a miniature train that circles around Peanuts Playground. All activities in the playground are reserved for those under 54in.

10
Challenge Park

Challenge Park is located in the back by Magnum (outside the park). Each attraction in Challenge Park requires a separate fee and does not require a Cedar Point ticket. In general Challenge Park opens one hour after the park and remains open for one hour past Cedar Point's listed closing time. To get to Challenge Park exit the park near Magnum - Challenge Park is right outside the gate.

Challenge Golf

Challenge golf is two 18-hole miniature golf courses. Each side offers many unique (and challenging) holes. Situated around a 30 foot tall mountain, the courses features caves, sand traps, hills and plenty of close calls with the many streams and ponds!

✓ Family

Prices are as follows: $5.95 for 18 holes, $7.95 for 36 holes. For those under 48 inches tall or over the age of 62 the price for 18 holes is $2.95.

Challenge Raceway

For speedy go-cart action, head right on over to Challenge Raceway. Challenge Raceway is made up of two different go-cart tracks. The Grand Prix Karts are for people who are over 16 years of age. Sprint Karts are for anyone over 48 inches tall.

Prices are as follows: Grand Prix 1 trip - $4.95, 2 trips - $7.95; Spirit Karts 1 trip - $4.95, 2 trips - $7.95.

Ripcord

Ever wonder what it would be like to fly, or to jump off a cliff? Well Ripcord comes close to both of those things. Ripcord is, perhaps, the scariest ride at Cedar Point. Riders strap into a harness (which is similar to a vest) and are attached to a big steel cable. The cable slowly pulls the rider(s) backward up into the sky. Once the rider(s) are lifted to the top (150 feet in the air), they are told via a loud speaker to pull the ripcord. The ripcord is a small rope on their harness that, when pulled, starts the ride. Riders will plummet and soar with speeds reaching 50 mph. After a minute of flying through the air, riders are slowed to a stop. For the most incredible experience of your life, ride Ripcord. Up to three people can fly Ripcord at once, and flyers must be at least 48in. tall. Reservations are suggested. To make one call 419-626-0830.

Prices are as follows (and are per person): If one person is flying alone: $30.00, if two people are flying: $22.00, if three people are flying together: $15.00.

X-Treme Trampoline

X-Treme Trampoline allows guests to experience what zero-gravity would feel like. While being strapped to a bungee cord system guests can jump as high as 24 feet in the air and do all the flips and tricks their heart desires. To use the X-Treme Trampoline guests must be between 30-200 pounds. To take part in the attraction the cost is $7.00.

11
Soak City

S oak City is Cedar Point's very own waterpark. Opened in 1988, Soak City has grown over the years into one of the biggest waterparks in the state of Ohio. Admission to Soak City is separate from Cedar Point and requires a different ticket.

Soak City is located near and around Magnum XL 200. If you are in Cedar Point, exit at the Magnum/Resort Gate (remember Soak City is a separate price). If you are driving to Soak City, you must take Perimeter Road to the back of the peninsula. To do that, when you get to the tollbooths, go to the largest one (which is on the far left side) and tell them you are going to Soak City. Once on Perimeter Road, take it until you are in the big parking lot facing Magnum and park in that lot.

Planning a visit

Soak City is open daily from Memorial Day weekend through Labor Day weekend. Hours vary, but generally the park opens at 10 or 11am and stays open until 7,8, or 9pm, which is plenty of time to take in all the attractions that Soak City offers. In general it takes three to four hours (maybe sometime alittle longer on the weekends in the summer due to large crowds) to experience everything Soak City has to offer.

 Coolers (and picnics) are not allowed inside Soak City. There is, however, a large picnic shelter outside the northern entrance to the park in which coolers and picnics are allowed.

Be sure to leave the goggles at home! They are not allowed on any attractions in Soak City. Life vests are available along with different swimming gear at the gift shop inside the park. Also don't forget the sunscreen! There are literally only a hand full of trees in the entire park so you will be soaking up plenty of the sun.

Inside the Park

Soak City has many waterslides, two inner tube rivers, two kiddy areas, and a large wave pool. Zoom Flume is a fun raft ride that the whole family will enjoy. The ride starts 76ft. in the air and works its way back to earth through a series of fast turns and short dips. When asked, most people say Zoom Flume is their favorite attraction in the park. Eerie Falls, like the name suggests, is not your average waterslide - it is three waterslides that are enclosed, making them quite dark so you never know where you will be headed next! What is a waterpark without a large wavepool? Soak City calls their massive 250,000 gallon wavepool Breakers Bay.

Another classic waterpark attraction (and the author's personal favorite) is the lazy river. Soak City doesn't just have one, they have two! Renegade River is a twisted version of the classic "lazy river" attraction. It features a mini wave pool, geysers, and buckets of water that spill on riders' heads. Then of course there is the classic "lazy river" attraction that encircles one whole section of the park.

Plenty is available for the young ones. There are two kiddy areas featuring kiddy versions of the water slides. The recently added Splash Zone is an interactive water play area filled with various water gadgets.

If you are over 21, Soak City has something just for you - a swim-up bar located in the middle of an adult only pool. Bubbles Swim-Up Bar is a perfect place for adults to unwind and forget about their problems.

Soak City doesn't have much to offer in the food/shopping department. There is one food stand, offering pizza, burgers, etc., located near the main entrance gate. Also located throughout the parks there are several small food stands that sell Dippin' Dots, beverages, etc.

Section 3

Outside the Park

12
Accommodations

W ith Cedar Point becoming more of a destination and not just .
an average amusement park, the need to spend the night in the
area is a growing issue. Cedar Point owns and operates three
hotels, an indoor waterpark resort, and a campground (complete with cabins
and cottages). The surronding cities are home to plenty of hotels, including
two indoor waterpark resorts. This chapter is broken up into three sections: the
Cedar Point owned hotels, the surounding areas hotels and a section on the
three indoor waterpark resorts.

Cedar Point Owned Resorts

Cedar Point owns and operates three hotels: Hotel Breakers, Sandcastle Suites, and Breakers Express, the campground Camper Village, and the
waterpark resort Castaway Bay. For more information on Cedar Point's hotels
and/or to make reservations call (419) 626-0830. Reservations can also be
placed online at CedarPoint.com To book a room at a Cedar Point resort, one
must atleast 21 years of age.

A hotel reservation desk is located on the east end of the main ticket
area at the front of the park. At the desk you may make a reservation for any

Cedar Point hotel, and/or "remote" check into Breakers Express.

Cedar Point resort guests receive several perks, including admission into the park 30 mins. early to ride select rides (changes each year, but usually includes two or three marquee rides) and the chance to purchase discounted park tickets.

Courtesy Vans are provided for guests staying at the marina, campground and all (Cedar Point owned) hotels. Courtesy vans pick up and drop off at the following locations: The pool in Lighthouse Point, Camper Village store, Breakwater Café, Sandcastle Suites' main lobby, Challenge Park/Soak City/Resort Entrance into Cedar Point (the stop is located just south-west of Challenge Golf), Hotel Breaker's main lobby, Marina Entrance (into Cedar Point)/Marina Store/Famous Daves/Bay Habour, Main Entrance Gate (stop is to the left of the gate near Blue Streak (turnaround) and Pet Chek).

The only place to find discounts on Cedar Point owned hotels is by getting the Getaway Guide. It is a magazine like **$$$** brochure about Cedar Point and features plenty of coupons. To receive it call 1-800-Best-Fun. Also from time to time, usually early or late into the season, Cedar Point.Com sometimes run hotel specials.

Breakers Express

Breakers Express could be billed as Cedar Point's attempt at building a Best Western or any other standard, no frills, hotel. Breakers Express, which has over 200 rooms, is located "off-Point" at the entrance to the causeway. The hotel is shaped in a giant "U", and for the price you can not go wrong. In the middle of the "U" is a pool in the shape of Snoopy. Each room features two double beds. Breakers Express offers a free continental breakfast.

Camper Village

Camper Village is Cedar Point's campground, and is located in the back of the peninsula near Soak City. While most of the "village's" land has been converted into Lighthouse Point, Camper Village still offers those with RVs a simple and affordable place to setup camp.

Lighthouse Point is a mini-resort in the northern portion of the Cedar Point peninsula. Cabins and cottages along with "luxury" RV sites, a pool, a pier, and an outdoor recreation area make up Lighthouse Point. The cottages and cabins have a living room, bedroom, kitchenette, and a bathroom.

They also have a walkout patio, with a grill. The cottages are situated along the coast of Lake Erie, while the cabins are located in the middle of the resort along a stream.

The campsites at Lighthouse Point include cable (TV) and electrical hookup. Please note that you cannot use tents at Lighthouse Point or Camper Village.

Hotel Breakers

Just a few feet away from the park and Lake Erie is Cedar Point's largest and oldest hotel – Hotel Breakers. Opened in 1905, Hotel Breakers is a turn of the century hotel. Over the years, additions were built and Breakers now has over 500 rooms.

Room types range from a regular hotel room to a Snoopy room to a suite. Prices start at $125 dollars and go up to $1000 dollars (for the presidental suite!). We recommend calling the park or carefully making your reservation online - while all the rooms are clean and nice, the kinds of rooms offered at the Breakers is huge. There is an older wing of the hotel with small rooms, a whole tower filled with suites, and even a conceirge floor. So be sure you know exactly what you are getting when you book as there several different kinds of rooms offered.

There are two outdoor pools and one indoor pool, plus the sandy Lake Erie beach is just steps from the hotel. Inside the Hotel Breakers there is a TGI Fridays, Coffee Shop, and an Italian restaurant. There is an ice cream parlor located next to one of the outside pools, which is a perfect place for a midday snack even if you are not a guest of the hotel.

Sandcastle Suites

At the northeastern tip of the Cedar Point peninsula Sandcastle Suites provides a quiet retreat from the action in the park. Surrounded by water on one side and trees encircling it on the others, Sandcastle Suites makes you feel like you're on an island far away from everything. The view cannot get any better. Rooms offer a gorgeous view of Lake Erie. If you are not one for scenery, you can get a room that overlooks Magnum's turnaround. Every room is a suite and accommodates up to 6 people. Each room has air conditioning, balcony or patio, small refrigerator, and a TV (color). There are tennis courts located next to the hotel. Despite being right on the water swimming is suggested near Hotel Breakers instead due to the rocky-ness of the beach by Sandcastle Suites.

While the name suites suggest some lavish rooms, the rooms are simple and clean. The selling point with Sandcastle Suites is the location. The view from the rooms that face the lake provide one of the best views out of any hotel in the area.

Comparsion

Below is a comparison chart of the three Cedar Point owned hotels (the fourth Cedar Point hotel - Castaway Bay is listed with the indoor waterparks later in the chapter). One word to note: Hotel Breakers has many different varieties of room types making it hard to compare to the other hotels. It features some old style rooms that are pretty small (the cheap rooms) yet it also offers some very nice suites.

Hotel Comparsion			
	Breakers Express	Hotel Breakers	Sandcastle Suites
Location	Off-point	On-point	On-point
Suites Available	No	Yes	All rooms
Pool	Outdoor	2 - outdoor, 1 - indoor	1- outdoor
Price	$60 - $200	$95 - $588	$135 - $355

Cedar Point Marina

Located on the west side (Sandusky Bay side) of the Cedar Point peninsula, the Cedar Point Marina is one of the largest on the Great Lakes with over 665 slips.

• Seasonal packages available
• The Marina monitors marine radio channel 16
• For Marina information call on Marine channel 9
• Reservations are taken with at least 48 hours advance notice.

The marina is home to two restruants and is a great place to escape to and take a break from the park for some food. Bay Harbor offers fresh seafood. Located on the Sandusky Bay side of Cedar Point near the Marina, Bay Harbor offers a great view along with good food. Famous Daves, a chain restruant known for their ribs, is located on a pier in the marina. To visit either restruant exit the park through the Marina gate or take the courtesy van to the Marina Gate. Bay Harbor and Famous Daves is located just feet from the Marina Gate.

Indoor Waterpark Resorts

Since 2001 the Sandusky area has become home to several indoor waterpark resorts. What's an indoor waterpark resort you ask? It is a large hotel with restaurants, aracades and other attractions, and of course and large indoor waterpark. Currently there are three in the Sandusky area: Castaway Bay, a tropical themed resorted owned by Cedar Point, Great Wolf Lodge, a northern-woods style lodge, and Kalahari, the largest hotel in Ohio and home to the largest indoor waterpark. With the sucess of the current three, several more resorts are on the drawing table and are expected to open in the next few years.

Castaway Bay

In the late 90s Cedar Point bought the upscale Radisson hotel near the entrance to Cedar Point. To rebrand the hotel under the Cedar Point name and renovate it, Cedar Point used the opportunity to turn it into Castaway Bay in late 2004. The entire hotel was remodeled, restaurant were rethemed, and a large indoor waterpark was added.

Castaway Bay may be located in Sandusky, but walking into the lobby guests are immediately transported to the tropics thanks to a big pirate ship in the lobby. All 237 rooms are also themed with tropical decor.

The waterpark is 38,000 square feet of warm, tropical, waterpark fun. Just how warm? Everyday the waterpark reaches a temperature 80 degrees. The Castaway Bay Wave Pool, a 100,000-gallon pool, generates ocean like waves while Cargo Cove is a giant pool for more swimming fun. Creature Cove is another pool with basketball hoops for those who like to swim and shoot!

For kids, there is a giant water playhouse called Lookout Lagoon which features a giant bucket on the top which dumps water on those unlucky souls below. There are also four "family size" slides and three body slides. What's a waterpark without a hot tub? Castaway Bay has a indoor/outdoor hot tub - yes the hot tub starts inside and connects to an outside hot tub (which is open year-round!).

Without doubt the marquee attraction of the park is Rendezvous Run. It is a waterslide with roller coaster like characteristics. Riders sit in inner tubes and, unlike tradiontal waterslides where the you only go downward during the entire ride, on Rendezvous Run you go up and down. Riders will go down one hill and, thanks to high pressured water, the tube is pushed quickly back up another hill.

The waterpark is not the only thing you'll find at Castaway Bay. Crabbie's Quarterdeck Arcade is home to everyone's favorite arcades games and is located right next to the waterpark. The Spa at Castaway Bay provides all your favorite spa treatments from facials to manicures and everything in between for both men and women. There is also a full service hair salon on site. Reservations are recommend. If you have any questions or would like make a reservation your spot call 419-625-5772.

No one should ever go hungry at Castaway Bay. The hotel is home to fives eateries The signature restaurant is the newly remodeled TGI Fridays. Mango Mike's is a buffet style eatery which is open for breakfast, lunch (brunch on Sunday), and dinner. The Snack Shack, located inside the waterpark, offers hot dogs, pizza, sandwiches and more. Gil's Lookout Lounge overlooks the harbor and offers pizza and sandwiches. Ebb & Eddy's is a small snack shop located near the main lobby with everything from Starbucks coffee to Krispy Kreme donuts.

For more information on Castaway Bay log on to CastawayBay. com or call 419-627-2500. Room rates range from $201 - $362 depending on the season and room type.

Great Wolf Lodge

Great Wolf Lodge, originally named the Great Bear Lodge, opened in 2001 and was the first indoor waterpark in the state. Located on Route 250, rougly five miles south of Cedar Point, Great Bear Lodge is located in the heart of the city's business distrct.

Great Wolf Lodge is themed around the idea of the "wilderness" It has 271 rooms, all of which are nonsmoking suites featuring high speed internet access, wet bar with microwave, pay-per-view movies/Nintnedo, a fridge, coffee maker, and hair dryer. The rooms (there are seven types) range from a standard suite to a two-story loft fireplace suite. One of the more popular rooms is called the "Kid Cabin Suite" which features a "mini cabin" in the middle of the room for the kids. The "mini cabin" has bunkbeds and a TV. A two night mininum may apply for weekends, holidays, and "premium periods." Check-in is at 4pm, while check-out is 11am.

The lodge does a great job with themeing. From the oustide of the lodge the entire complex looks like a giant log cabin. The theme is carried throughtout the hotel with a heavily themed lobby right down to the decor in the room. The only downside is the fact that the lodge is located literally right between a mall and a large shopping store. That takes away slightly from the wilderness feel - but the inside nearly makes up for it.

The waterpark has a large variety of slides, pools, play equipment, and even has a short lazy river. At the center of the waterpark, which is kept at a comfortable 82 degrees, is Fort Mackenzie, a large play structure with 'numerous water contraptions and a bucket above that dumps water on the

Did You KNOW...
Building Millennium Force and the Great Wolf Lodge cost the same price - $25 million dollars

people below. For those who enjoy waterslides, the waterpark is home to many of all sizes - ranging from short, kid-sized ones, to ones that start at the ceiling of the waterpark and even go outside (don't worry they are enclosed) before ending up in a pool. The waterpark also features a pool with basketball hoops and numerous attractions for the little ones. Called "Bear Track Landing", the area features many fountains and shallow pools filled with different water contraptions - all geared for the youngest children. During the summer months Raccoon Lagoon opens. Raccoon Lagoon is an entire outdoor area complete with pools, water basketball, patio areas, and an outdoor bar.

Besides the waterpark, the Great Wolf Lodge offers plenty more. The Northern Lights Arcade is a large aracade with all sorts of games. The lodge is also home to three gift shops: Northwoods Exposures, a small shop that focuses on photo products, Buckhorn Exchange, a large gift shop located near the main lobby, and Bear Essentials, a small shop located inside the waterpark which focuses on swimming products. There are three places that serve food in the lodge. Gitchigoomie Grill, a northern-Canadian themed restrauant. Klondike Cafe, a quick-service food outlet located in the waterpark and Lum-

ber Jack's Cook Shanty, a lumber jack themed home style cooking restruant.
For more information contact the Great Wolf Lodge:
- http://www.greatwolflodge.com/
- 888.779.2327

Kalahari

Kalahari is much different than both Castaway Bay and Great Wolf Lodge in its size and theme. Kalahari, the largest of the three (actually the largest indoor water park in the state), is located about 15 minutes south of Cedar Point along Rte. 250. Themed around the African sanvanna and dessert, Kalahari offers much more than just an indoor water park - there is even a rope bridge to get to the lobby!

With 596 rooms Kalahari is not only the largest hotel in the area but with its' new expansion will become the largest hotel in the state. Each room is unqiuely themed to the african savanna and makes guests really feel as if they are in Africa and not Ohio (the resort really does a great job with themeing). In early 2007 the resort announced plans to add 96 condos (or as they call them "kondos") to the resort.

The indoor water park is clearly Kalahari's marquee attraction. The park features a great mix of both kids attractions and thrilling water park attractions. Crocodile Cove is nearly 3,000 square foot pool with basketball hoops and water cannons. A 920 foot long lazy river is a perfect place to relax but watch out for the waterfalls and geysers. Leopard's Lair is a perfect place for the little ones as the water in the pool is less than one foot deep. It also features numerous water guns and slides. Swahili Swirl is a nearly 400ft long tube slide while Victoria Falls is a family sized raft slide and a great family attraction.

The two most best known attractions at Kalahari are the watercoaster and the FlowRider. The watercoaster is not your average water slide - its a roller coaster with water. Instead of riders sliding downward the whole time, the tube actually has hills (it propells rafts up the hills using conveyor belts) to create a longer, more thrilling water slide experience. The FlowRider, which is unique to Kalahari, allows guests to try their hands at surfing a fake five-foot wall. Using over 50,000 gallons of water per minute, FlowRider allows guest to surf or bodyboard in a safe yet thrilling environment. Lessons are available (for a price). See the water park front desk for more information.

The waterpark is not the only attraction at Kalahari. Madagascar Mini-Golf is a miniature golf course located inside allowing the challenge of mini-golf year around. Tree Top Play is an indoor playground area designed with the young ones in mind. Pottery Pizzaz allow those intrested in pottery to try their hand at pottery. Kalahari also has a large aracade. There is also a newly opened convention center.

Kalahari is unqiue in many ways. By the time this book hits the shelve Kalahari will be the largest hotel in the state of Ohio and one of the largest indoor waterparks in the world.

For more information contact the Kalahari:
- http://www.kalahariresort.com
- 1-877-KALAHARI

The Future

No, thats not the name of the lastest waterpark! As this book goes to print the indoor waterpark boom created by Great Wolf Lodge and fueled by Castaway Bay and Kalahari is in full gear. An entire resort is proposed for an area near Kalahari called Shipwreck Falls. Another resort is in the planning stages for the Port Clinton/Marblehead area. The future of Sandusky is quite exciting as it appears the area will just keep growing with more and more to do.

Other hotels in the area

Cedar Point has created quite a hotel market in Sandusky and the surrounding area. Within 15 miles of the park there are roughly 50 hotels to choose from. Most are just standard chain hotels with basic amenities, though in recent years hotels have been built with suites and more upscale rooms. Most of the rooms are found along Route 250 - the main road that connects the turnpike and Route 2 to Cedar Point. On weekends, during the summer, and over holidays many, if not most, of the hotels in the city become booked up, therefore it would be best to book in advance. From our research it is hard to walk-in and try to get a discount. Most of the hotels are only open during the Cedar Point seasovn so they are reluctant to give many discounts and most of the hotels are generally priced about the same.

Many hotels offer guests a chance to buy discounted Cedar Point tickets. Several hotels have their own shuttle service to and from Cedar Point. From our experiences with the various shuttles, most of them seem to be quite reliable. If you get a chance to use a shuttle, we recommend it. It will save you from paying the $10 dollar parking fee at the park! For those under 21 who wish to spend the night - do some research! Many hotels, including all the Cedar Point owned ones, require someone over 21 to be present at check-in. With that said there are several hotels that do allow 18 year olds to check in. We would list the hotels but they seem to change their policies often so its best just to call the hotel itself.

On the following page is a list of a select number of hotels near Cedar Point (see locations - some are located up to 15 mins away). By no means is this a complete list or an endorsement of any kind, it is simply provided as a refrence and as a starting point for trip planning.

Best Budget Inn North 2027 Cleveland Rd. Sandusky, OH. 44870	http://www.sanduskybestbudget.com 419-626-3610
Best Budget Inn South 5918 Milan Rd. Sandusky, OH. 44870	http://www.sanduskyhotels.com 419-625-7252
Best Western Cedar Point 1530 Cleveland Rd. Sandusky, OH. 44870	http://www.bestwestern.com/cedar-pointarea 419-625-9234
Clarion Inn-Sandusky 1119 Sandusky Mall Blvd. Sandusky, OH. 44870	http://www.sanduskyhotels.com 419-625-6280
Comfort Inn-Maingate 1711 Cleveland Rd. Sandusky, OH. 44870	http://www.sanduskyhotels.com 419-625-4700
Comfort Inn-Sandusky 5909 Milan Rd. Sandusky, OH. 44870	http://www.sanduskyhotels.com 419-621-0200
Comfort Inn 11020 Milan Rd. Milan, OH. 44846	http://www.sanduskyhotels.com 419-499-4681
Comfort Suites 6011 Milan Rd. Sandusky, OH. 44870	http://www.sanduskyhotels.com 419-617-9595

Days Inn-Central 4315 Milan Rd. Sandusky, OH. 44870	http://www.cedarpointareahotels.com 419-627-8884
Days Inn-South Turnpike 11410 US. Rt. 250 Milan, OH. 44846	http://www.daysinn.com 419-499-4961
Econo Lodge 1904 Cleveland Rd. Sandusky, OH. 44870	http://www.cedarpointareahotels.com 419-627-8000
Econo Lodge-South 3309 Milan Rd. Sandusky, OH. 44870	http://www.cedarpointareahotels.com 419-626-8720
Fairfield Inn 6220 Milan Rd. Sandusky, OH. 44870	http://www.cedarpointareafairfield.com 419-621-9500
Hampton Inn 6100 Milan Rd. Sandusky, OH. 44870	http://www.hamptoninn.com 419-609-9000
Holiday Inn Holidome 5513 Milan Rd. Sandusky, OH. 44870	http://www.staysandusky.com 419-626-6671
Knights Inn 2405 Cleveland Rd. Sandusky, OH. 44870	http://www.mhdcorp.com 419-621-9000
LaQuinta Inn 3304 Milan Rd. Sandusky, OH. 44870	http://www.lq.com 419-626-6766
Microtel Inn 601 Rye Beach Rd. Huron, OH. 44839	http://www.huronmicrotel.com 419-433-7829
Motel 6 11406 U.S. Rt. 250 Milan, OH. 44846	http://www.motel6-sandusky-milan. com 419-499-8001
Quality Inn & Suites 1935 Cleveland Rd. Sandusky, OH. 44870	http://www.cedarpointareahotels.com 419-626-6761
Ramada Inn 5608 Milan Rd. Sandusky, OH. 44870	http://www.sanduskyhotels.com 419-626-9890

Rodeway Inn-North 1021 Cleveland Rd. Sandusky, OH. 44870	http://www.cedarpointareahotels.com 419-626-6852
Rodeway Inn-Sandusky 2905 Milan Rd. Sandusky, OH. 44870	http://www.sanduskyhotels.com 419-625-1291
Super 8 5410 Milan Rd. Sandusky, OH. 44870	http://www.sanduskysuper8.com 419-625-7070
Travelodge 5906 Milan Rd. Sandusky, OH. 44870	http://www.sanduskyhotels.com 419-627-8971

13
Local Area

Cedar Point is located in Sandusky, Ohio (Elevation: 584 ft., Population: 29,764). Voted one of the best small cites in America and one of the best places to retire, Sandusky and the surrounding area is home to a lot more than just Cedar Point. Filled with museums, golf courses, and more, the area is a great place to have some extra fun. Just northwest of Sandusky is a chain of islands that are known throughout the midwest for their fishing, partying and natural beauty.

Before leaving for the Sandusky area, logging onto FunCoast.Com (http://www.funcoast.com) is a must. The site offers an up-to-date calendars of events not just for Sandusky but also the islands and surrounding areas. The site, which is owned by the local newspaper and billed as an online entertainment guide, also features photos, feature articles, visitor guides and much more.

This chapter is divided into four main sections - general area information, local attractions, the Lake Erie Islands and a guide on the ferry services offered in the area.

Getting More Information

Contact the Sandusky Area Visitor's Bureau at
- http://www.sanduskyohiocedarpoint.com/
- 1-800-255-3743

Getting Around

- Advanced Limo: 419-447-5466
- Sandusky Main Street Trolley is a trolley (actually a bus made to look like a trolley) that runs from various stops along Rte. 250 back and forth to downtown Sandusky. It operates from Memorial Day through Labor Day. For more information call 419-627-0740 or log onto http://www.sanduskymainstreet.com

Area Attractions

African Safari Wildlife Park

Located in Port Clinton, OH. (roughly 20 mins. West of Cedar Point) African Safari Wildlife Park provides guests which a chance to get up close and personal to its collection of exotic animals. Unlike most other wildlife parks this park is a drive-thru safari. Besides the drive-thru safari there are camel and pony rides, shows, and a restaurant.

- 1-800-521-2660
- www.africansafariwildlifepark.com

Cedar Downs

Located in the Quality Inns & Suites (roughly one minute from Cedar Point) Cedars Downs offers off-track gaming and entertainment. Besides the gaming there is bowling and an arcade.

- 1-800-654-3364
- www.cedarpointareahotels.com

Edison's Birthplace

Even Thomas Edison liked the Sandusky area! Ok, so maybe the liked part is a stretch but Edison was indeed born, in 1847, just a few miles south of Cedar Point. Visitors can tour his childhood home and learn about his greatest accomplishments.

Ghostly Manor

Rated as one of the top ten walkthrough haunted attractions in the US, Ghostly Manor provides more than just haunting experiences. Ghostly Manor constantly updates their haunted house to feature the lastest technology and new props. The haunted house is not the only thrill-filled experience. New for 2006, Ghostly Manor added Ohio's first and only "XD-3d Theatre."

- 419-625-9935
- http://www.ghostlymanor.com

Goofy Golf

Goofy Golf is a family entertainment center located on Route 250 roughly 5 minutes south of Cedar Point. It is composed of two 18-hole mini-golf courses, bumper boats, three go-kart tracks, and an arcade.

- 419-625-9935
- http://www.goofygolf.net

Maritime Museum

Take a seat back in time, and learn about Sandusky's maritime history. The museum features countless displays on the area's rich history. Located just across the bay from Cedar Point, it uses numerous photos and artifacts to tell visitors about the area's maritime past.

- 419-624-0274
- http://www.sanduskymaritime.org

Merry-Go-Round Museum

One of the most unique and enjoyable museums around, the Merry-Go-Round Museum features displays on Merry-Go-rounds and carousels and is even home to an operating antique carousel. Located in downtown roughly five minutes from Cedar Point, the Merry-Go-Round is a perfect addition to any trip or a great place to spend a rainy day. Visitors can watch carvers at work on new horses, and learn about carousel history and the organ music associated with it. Admission is five dollars for adults, four dollars for guests age 60 or older, and three dollars for children age four-fourteen (children under the age of three are free). Best of all a ride on the carousel is included in the admission price!

- 419-626-611
- http://www.merrygoroundmuseum.org

Monsoon Lagoon

Located in Port Clinton (roughly a 25 min. drive west of Cedar Point) Monsoon Lagoon is a water park and family fun park. Attractions include a lazy river, adult pool with swim-up bar, kids squirt zone, large interactive water fort playground, and waterslides. In the family fun center of the complex there is mini-golf, bumper boats, an aracade, and go carts.

- 419-732-6671
- http://www.monsoonlagoonwaterpark.com

Norwalk Raceway Park

Thirty minutes south of Cedar Point is the Norwalk Raceway Park. Looking at or riding Top Thrill Dragster do you wonder what a real drag race is like? Just head on over to Norwalk Raceway Park. Drag races are held every Wednesday, Friday, Saturday and Sunday. The quarter mile track sees cars racing down at speeds over 200 miles per hour! The track which tries to be family friendly has a playground for kids and hosts kids events at various times throughout the year.

- 419-668-5555
- http://www.norwalkraceway.com

Prehistoric Forest & Mystery Hill

Prehistoric Forest is a forest filled with large models of dinos, an archeo-dig site, a large "volcano", and a mini-golf course. Mystery Hill is a magic lovers paradise. Can you explain how things go against the laws of physics? Both attractions are located in Marblehead - a 25 minute drive from Cedar Point (despite being right on the other side of the bay!).

- 419-798-5230
- http://www.prehistoricforest.com

Lake Erie Islands

Besides Cedar Point, the areas biggest summertime draw is a group of islands located northwest of the park. Just how popular are the islands? According to the county's vistitors bureau the year round population of the county is roughly 41,000, while on a weekend in the summer the population soars to over 250,000 people! The area is known as the "The Walleye Capital of the World."

Put-in-Bay

Put-in-Bay, located on South Bass Island, is a popular island destination that attracts thousands of visitors each year because of the island's history, fishing, attractions, and nightlife. The island first became famous as it played an important part in the War of 1812 when Commander Perry used the port as a place to set up his troops during a battle on Lake Erie.

The island's attractions include mini-golf, Perry's Victory and International Peace Memorial (one of the nation's tallest memorials), a train tour, parasailing, golf, a cave, and much more. The island is known for its nightlife and is in fact home to a restruant that, according to the Guiness Book of World Records, features the world's longest bar.

For more information on Put-in-Bay call the visitors bureau at 419-285-2832. There are also a number of online guides to the area (links are posted below):

- http://www.put-in-bay.com/
- http://www.putinbay.com/

Kellys Island

Kelleys Island, another Lake Erie island, is actually the largest American island in Lake Erie. It is known for fishing and its breathtaking natural beauty. The island is home to the 600-acre Kelleys Island State Park. Fishing is big here – in fact Kelleys Island is known by fishermen as the "Walleye Capital of the World." The island also features a downtown area with mini golf, restaurants, and more.

For more information call the chamber of commerce at 419 746-2360 or visit their website at http://www.kelleysislandchamber.com

Water Transportation

Cars are not the only way to get from Sandusky to the Lake Erie islands. There are several ferry services from the different islands to various points along the coast, including Sandusky. We recommend calling ahead, especially if you plan to use their services in the off-season, as some may run limited or no boats.

Jet Express

Known for their high-speed boats, Jet Express travels between Sandusky and Port Clinton. Jet Express also operates a line from Port Clinton to Kellys Island and Put-in-Bay. They specalize in both early and late in the day services.

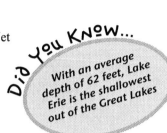

Did You Know...

With an average depth of 62 feet, Lake Erie is the shallowest out of the Great Lakes

- 1-800-245-1538
- http://www.jet-express.com

Kellys Island Ferry Boat Lines

Like the company's name suggests, Kellys Island Ferry Boat Lines specializes in both passenger and car transportation between Kellys Island and Marblehead.
- 419-798-9763
- http://www.kellysislandferry.com

Miller Boat Line

Miller Boat Line offers both passenger and car transportation between Catawba, Put-in-Bay and Middle Bass Island.
- 1-800-500-2421
- http://www.millerferry.com

MV Jiimaan

One of the lesser known ferry operators is the MV Jiimaan but that is in part due to the unique service between Sandusky and Ontario, Canada that they offer. The ferry also makes stops in Leamington, Kingsville and at Pelee Island. The line is in operation from April through mid-December. If you are interested in traveling between the Canada and the U.S. we recommend you call adhead to confirm the current boarder crossing procedures.

- 1-800-661-2220
- http://www.ontarioferries.com/jii/english/index.html

14
Fun Chapter

D o you enjoy Cedar Point? Well, you're not the only one – there are hundreds of Cedar Point enthusiasts, and thousands upon thousands of roller coaster fans. This chapter is geared to those who wants to know how to best experience the thrills of the rides at Cedar Point.

Where To Start - Rides

The following list is in order from the mildest to the wildest coaster:

1. Jr. Gemini – Great beginner coaster - not very intense.

2. Woodstock's Express – Slightly taller and faster then Jr. Gemini – and provides more turns.

3. Cedar Creek Mine Ride – Overall not very intense but features several fast moments.

4. Iron Dragon – Taller and faster than Cedar Creek Mine Ride, and the cars swing.

5. Disaster Transport – Not much taller or faster than Iron Dragon, but with the ride being in the dark it can be a little bit scarier.

6. Blue Streak – It isn't very tall, but it is fast. This is the first coaster on the list that provides airtime, which some people don't like.

7. Corkscrew – Corkscrew is one of the smaller roller coasters and is not very intense. This is a great ride to see how people handle going upside down.

8. Wildcat – Offers many fast turns and steep drops that can catch people off guard.

9. Gemini – Gemini is the first "bigger" coaster. It is tall and fast but is not very intense.

10. Mean Streak – Mean Streak may look big and bad, but looks can be deceiving. When the ride first opened it was "mean", but over the years Cedar Point has slowed it down (by using brakes) thus making it less intense.

11. Magnum XL-200 – It has an "XL" in the name for a reason - it is extra large! The first drop isn't extremely intense nor is it very steep(compared to the newer coasters), while the second half of the ride features much, and airtime that may take first time riders off-guard.

12. Maverick - While it is hard to tell where Maverick will rank since this book has gone to print before the ride opened, based on the various ride elements and similar roller coasters, we think it would be right here on the list.

13. Raptor – The first drop may not appear to death-defying, but the ride is very disorienting due to the numerous inversions and sharp turns.

14. Mantis – Can you stand it? The first drop may be strange for newcomers because you are standing. The last part of the ride is very disorienting.

15. Wicked Twister – Launching forward and backward with a top speed reaching 72 mph may take the breath out of some – while the twists on the tower may disorient others.

16. Millennium Force – At 93 miles per hour, this 310-foot beast is the second most intense ride in the park. The first drop is out of this world. The rest of the ride is intense – how could it not be when the slowest speed is 50 mph? The worst part about Millennium Force is waiting in line.

17. Top Thrill Dragster – 420 feet tall, launch from 0-120 mph in four seconds – do I need to say more as to why Top Thrill Dragster is the most intense ride in the park?

Riding Tips

While a ride on any of Cedar Point's attractions might scare anyone, for those brave at heart we offer the following tips for the "scariest ride."

- Ride with your eyes closed – this means your body cannot see what is ahead.
- Ride while it's wet – though during heavy storms the rides will close, they remain open during light rain – which means slicker track, thus a faster ride. Plus, the rain makes it harder to see what's ahead.
- Night rides – many rides (or at least parts of them) are not totally lit up at night, meaning a ride on your favorite thrill ride may feel like you are flying through a dark abyss.
- Front vs. back: the ride may feel totally different depending on where you sit (see the ride tips below for some examples). Due to the design of most lift systems, the back of the train gets whipped over the hill (since the front of the train is already traveling down), while the front offers the best views.

Roller Coaster Fans

Think you are the only one that loves roller coasters? Think again! There are numerous clubs throughout the country with thousands of members who all love roller coasters. Below are a few of the more popular roller coaster clubs that have been around for a while and are worth checking out. Clubs usually put out a publication, have several events each year, and may get special discounts to parks or invitations to special events (i.e. CoasterMania). Joining a club is a great way to connect with fellow enthusiasts and offers a chance to make new friends.

- American Coaster Enthusiasts http://www.aceonline.org $60
- Great Ohio Coaster Club http://gocc.coasternewsnetwork.com $20
- Florida Coaster Club http://www.floridacoasterclub.com/ $20

• European Coaster Club http://www.coasterclub.org/ $41

$ = Cost of a regular, yearly membership

Trivia

Just how well do you know Cedar Point? Some of the questions below are easy, others are hard, but hopefully you'll learn a fun fact or two!

1. How many acres is Cedar Point?
2. What was Cedar Point's first roller coaster?
3. How many acres is Soak City?
4. What is the top speed of Mean Streak?
5. How many entrances into the park are there?
6. How many trash cans are on the Cedar Point peninsula?
7. What year was Cedar Fair L.P. formed?
8. How steep is Blue Streak's first drop?
9. How steep is the lift on Millennium Force?
10. What was the original name for Mantis?
11. In which year did HalloWeekends premier?
12. What year did Ocean Motion open?
13. How much is the causeway toll?
14. How many first aid stations are there?
15. What is the speed limit on Perimeter Road?
16. Blue Streak is named after what?
17. What was the first year of the Summer Spectacular?
18. What year did Helen Keller visit Cedar Point?
19. Which side on Gemini is longer?
20. Pay-One-Price started in what year?
21. What year did Camper Village open?
22. Where were the bumper boats originally located?
23. Since opening in 1964, to the nearest million, how many rides has Blue Streak given?
24. How many hotels does Cedar Point own and operate?
25. Where is the main telephone switchboard located?
26. Which ride is 19 feet high and travels at a top speed of 6 mph?
27. What park did Cedar Downs Racing Derby come from?
28. How many acres is the main parking lot?
29. In past years, from which park did Cedar Point buy a steam engine?
30. When did the first piece of steel for Millennium Force arrive at Cedar

Point?

31. Did a Cedar Point hotel ever have the recognition of being a "National Historic Place"?

32. Camper Village is in which geometric shape?

33. What does Jr. Gemini and Millennium Force have in common?

34. If you were to ride every roller coaster at Cedar Point once in a day, how many times would you have gone upside down?

35. Which is the biggest indoor waterpark in the Sandusky area?

36. How many coasters at the park are launched coasters?

37. How many locations in the park sell the famous Cedar Point french fries?

38. Roughly how many hundreds of support columns are used on Raptor?

39. If all the park's coasters were hooked together, how long would the track be?

Trivia - Answers!

1. 364 acres

2. Switchback Railway

3. 18 acres

4. 65-miles per hour

5. 4 entrances

6. Roughly 2000 trash cans

7. 1983

8. 45-degrees

9. 45-degrees

10. Banshee

11. 1997

12. 1981

13. 50 cents

14. 2 first aid stations

15. 23- mph

16. Sandusky High School Sports Teams

17. 1995

18. 1925

19. Blue side

20. 1970

21. 1971

22. Kiddy Kingdom

23. 51 million rides
24. 4 hotels and 1 campground
25. Hotel Breakers
26. Jr. Gemini
27. Euclid Beach Park
28. 64-acres
29. Disney
30. December 1998
31. Yes, the Hotel Breakers gained the status in 1981, but due to recent additions, it lost the status in 2001.
32. Two giant circles
33. They were both designed by Intamin
34. 16 times
35. Kalahari
36. 3 - Wicked Twister, Top Thrill Dragster and Maverick
37. 3 - Happy Friar, Hot Potato, Mr. Potato
38. 300 steel columns
39. 47,353 feet

F.A.Q

Does Cedar Point have a space problem? Is Cedar Point running out of room to expand?

Cedar Point has limited room due to its location, but there is not a space problem. In fact, there are numerous "open" areas throughout the peninsula. Some people also think Cedar Point is running out of room because the rides are "shoehorned", or built on top of each other. According to Cedar Point, some rides are "shoehorned" to bring more attention to the midway and to interact with guests.

Is the Magnum XL 200 sinking? Is it being sold?

The Magnum XL 200 is not sinking nor is it being sold. This rumor was started by many employees as an April Fools joke. Magnum is still one of the park's more popular rides and is voted over and over again as one of the best roller coasters in the world.

Why isn't Cedar Point open in the winter?
Being out on the pennisula during the winter is not fun at all. Thanks to the wind it is always much, much colder than it is on the mainland. The park did try a winter event in the early 90s called "Christmas in the Park" but the event wasn't well attended.

Who owns Cedar Point?
Cedar Point is owned and operated by Cedar Fair L.P. Cedar Fair is a publicly traded company on the New York Stock Exchange, Symbol: FUN.

Other Cedar Fair Parks

Cedar Point is owned and operated by Cedar Fair L.P. and Cedar Point is not alone. Cedar Fair operates twelve other amusement parks across the country and several waterparks. On the following pages is a brief description of each of the parks.

For those looking to add on to their Cedar Point vacation with another amusement park or two, be sure to read up on Geauga Lake & Kings Island. Both are great parks also located in Ohio.

Remember by buying a Cedar Fair MAXX Season Pass you can get unlimited access into most of the park below (all of the parks with the MAXX Plus pass). For more information on season passes see pages 18-19.

$$$

Bonfante Gardens
Location: Gilroy, CA. (Northern CA.)
Operating Season: April - Mid. Nov.

Having opened in 2001, Bonfante Gardens is one of the few completely new amusement parks to open in the country in recent years. While the park is smaller in scale than most amusment parks the nineteen rides are very family friendly. The most popular attraction is the Quicksilver Express Mine Coaster that speeds around a hill and through nearly 600 trees! Speaking of trees, Bonfante Gardens is best known for its incredible landscaping. The park appears to be a giant garden show with nearly every square inch of the park filled with beautiful flowers, bushes and trees - creating an incredible atmosphere.
• 404-840-7100
• http://www.bonfantegardens.org

Canada's Wonderland

Location: Vaughan, ON. (Northwest suburb of Toronto)
Operating Season: May - Early Oct.

Orginally known as Paramount's Canada's Wonderland, Cedar Fair acquired the park in mid-2006. The park is one of the largest in Canada and has a collection of 14 roller coasters including the popular Italian Job: Stunt Track coaster and the inverted coaster Top Gun. The park also has a large collection of family rides and several areas just for kids, including Nickelodeon Central.

For more information:
- 905-832-7000
- http://www.canadas-wonderland.com

Carowinds

Location: Charlotte, NC.
Operating Season: Late March - Oct.

Carowinds, located in Charlotte, NC. is an 108-acre amusement and water park. The park is home to 60 rides, attractions and shows - 12 of which are roller coasters. Park highlights include BORG Assimilator - a flying coaster, Fairly Odd Coaster - a small wooden coaster themed around the cartoon with the same name, and Top Gun: The Jet Coaster - a highly rated inverted coaster.

Did You Know...
Despite being in North Carolina, a portion of the park actually extends into South Carolina!

For more information:
- 800-888-4FUN
- http://www.carowinds.com

Dorney Park

Location: Allentown, PA.
Operating Season: May - Oct.

Dorney Park, like Cedar Point, is one of the oldest amusement parks in the country having opened in 1884. Unqiuely built on and around a foothill of the mountains, Dorney Park is filled with attractions for all ages and includes a large water park called Wildwater Kingdom (included with admission to the amusement park). The park has eight roller coasters including the hyper roller coaster Steel Force, the floorless coaster Hydra (that features a loop between the station and the lift hill - only one like that in the world!), and the highly acclaimed inverted coaster Talon. The park also features many family rides including the classic, but nearly extinct, amusement ride the whip. It also has a Camp Snoopy area for the young ones. Wildwater Kingdom is a large, thrilling but family friendly water park that best of all is free with admission into Dorney Park!

> For more information:
> • 610-395-3724
> • http://www.dorneypark.com

Geauga Lake

Location: Aurora, OH. (subburb of Cleveland), just over an hour from CP
Operating Season: May - Sept.

    Orginally just a gathering spot for locals Geauga Lake slowly turned into an amusement park in the last century. Since 1889 people have gathered at the park and over time nine coasters and numerous thrill rides have been installed. In 2000 Six Flags branded the park "Six Flags Ohio" and added four roller coasters and a kids area. In 2001 the park purchased Sea World (which used to be located on the other side of the lake) and made both parks into one mega park called Six Flags World of Adventures. The owners tried to become Cedar Point biggest competition. In the late spring of 2004, just 30 days before the park opened for the season, Cedar Fair purchased the park and renamed it back to the orginal name - Geauga Lake. In those 30 days Cedar Fair had to rename many names (Six Flags owned the naming rights to rides such as Batman), replace signs and tried to make the park their own. Since then the park has seen an very unqiue transformation in which Cedar Fair is trying to "downsize" the park in the sense to return it to its roots as an normal amusement park and not some mega park like Six Flags tried. The park has also devolped an entirely new large waterpark where Sea World once stood called Wildwater Kingdom. It is included with admission into Geauga Lake. In early 2007 it was announced X-Flight, the park's flying coaster, would be headed to Kings Island.

    Geauga Lake is home to nine roller coasters, plenty of thrill rides, and numerous kids attractions. Park highlights include the Big Dipper roller coaster which was built in 1925, Dominator (formely known as Batman) a floorless coaster that loops and twists its way over the lake, and the Villan - a large twisted wooden roller coaster. Connecting the park with the former Sea World side is a large boardwalk that goes across the lake.

    Wildwater Kingdom is a semi-new 17 acre waterpark that includes a 30,000-square-foot wave pool. It also features numerous slides, a lazy river, and a water fort playground for the little ones.

      Geauga Lake is a unique park. What started out as a small, local destination was forced into "trying" to become a national destination under Six Flags management. That planned failed and the park is now slowly returning to its roots of a local-style amusement park. Don't let the local-style fool you, the park's collection of rides and its waterpark are above average and are worth the price of admission. It is a perfect side-trip from Cedar Point - especially if you have to pass through Cleveland to get to Cedar Point.

For more information:
- 330-562-7131
- http://www.geaugalake.com

Great America

Location: Santa Clara, CA. (near San Jose)
Operating Season: Late March - Oct.

      Orginally known as Paramount's Great America, Cedar Fair acquired the park in mid-2006. Located in Santa Clara, Great America is a midsize park that also has a water park - Boomerang Bay (included with the price of admission to Great America). The park features eight roller coasters and a large collection of thrill rides including one themed around the Survivor TV show. Nickelodeon Central and KidZville round out the park's collection and offers rides and shows for the little ones.

For more information:
- 408-988-1776
- http://www.pgathrills.com

Kings Dominion

Location: Doswell, VA.
Operating Season: Late March - Oct.

      Orginally known as Paramount's Kings Dominion, Cedar Fair acquired the park in mid-2006. Kings Dominion is a 400-acre theme park that has over 200 rides, attractions, and shows. The park has a collection 13 roller coasters, including the unique Volcano - The Blast Coaster that blasts riders into a volcano and then explodes (ok, launches, but explodes sounds better!) out of the top before twisting and turning all around the fake mountain. In addition to the coasters there are two children's areas and several thrill rides including one themed to the movie Tomb Raider. Included in the price of admission is WaterWorks, a 19-acre water park which is being expanded with three new attractions for the 2007 season.

For more information:
- 804-876-5561
- http://www.kingsdominion.com

Kings Island

Location: Kings Mill, OH. (Suburb of Cincinnati)
Operating Season: April - Oct.

Known most recently as Paramount's Kings Island, Cedar Fair acquired the park in mid-2006. Located northeast of Cincinnati, Kings Island is actually the most popular seasonal amusement park in the country and there is a good reason behind its popularity. The park has one of the best mixes of thrill rides and family rides. It has 13 coasters, including the famous wooden coaster the Beast, but six of them are family friendly (three of the six are especially family friendly and geared for the young ones). Nickelodeon Universe, an award winning kids' area, features over 18 rides and attractions designed with kids and families in mind. The park is also slowly trying to become a full-fledged resort destination. They recently added a Great Wolf Lodge resort near the park.

In recent years Kings Island completlely revamped their water park and branded it under the name Boomerang Bay. Included in the price of admission into Kings Island, Boomerang Bay features all sorts of the latest slides and trends in water park activities. Attractions include Pipeline Paradise, which allows guest to grab a body board and hang ten as they try their body boarding skills; while Kookaburra Bay is a secluded lagoon with cascading waterfalls and in-water lounging.

Did You KNOW...
At 7359 feet in length the Beast is the longest coaster in the Western Hemisphere!

Boomerang Bay prides itself on offering guests the five-star treatment with live music, cabanas, lush landscaping, full bar facilities and much more.

For the 2007 season the park received the roller coaster X-Flight from Geauga Lake and renamed and rebranded it "Firehawk."

Kings Island is one of the nation's gems when it comes to amusement parks. From the kids areas to the roller coasters, it appears each area of the park is always winning an award for something. Coasters like the Beast make the park a must visit for any coaster fans.Tthe Nickelodeon areas make the park a huge hit and a must visit for families. Whether you are thinking about planning a separate trip or will be passing by the Cincinnati area on your way to Cedar Point - a stop at Kings Island will not disappoint.

For more information:
- 800-288-0808
- http://www.pki.com

Knott's Berry Farms

Location: Buena Park, CA. (Southern CA.)
Operating Season: Year-Around

Located just down the street from Disneyland, Knott's Berry Farms first opened in 1940. In the early 1980s Snoopy and the Peanuts gang became the park's mascot. Interestingly enough, when the park was bought by Cedar Fair in 1997 it allowed all the other Cedar Fair parks (including Cedar Point) to use the Peanuts gang(which Cedar Point did - less than two years after buying Knotts, Camp Snoopy was installed at Cedar Point). Over the years Knott's has turned into a well-known, complete amusement park with eight coasters and numerous rides. Park highlights include Xcelerator,which is a smaller version of Top Thrill Dragster, and GhostRider, which constantly ranks as one of the best wooden roller coasters in the world. The park is also filled with family rides including the area Camp Snoopy, from which the Cedar Point version is designed.

Due to its location near Disneyland, the park is often overlooked by tourists as just another amusement park. Knotts has something for everyone and is always highly rated as a park.

For more information:
- 714-220-5200
- http://www.knotts.com

Knott's Soak City

Location: Several parks throughout Southern California
Operating Season: Varies

Cedar Fair owns three water parks in the southern California area - all of which are called Knott's Soak City (yes, the name is based off the orginal Soak City at Cedar Point!). Each have different prices, hours and dates of operation, so it is best to check with each park before leaving home.

A website for all three can be found at: http://www.knotts.com/soakcity/
The parks, followed by their phone number, are listed below:
- Chula Vista - (619) 661-7373
- Right next to Knott's Berry Farm - (714) 220-5200
- Palm Springs - (760) 327-0499

Michigan's Adventure
Location: Muskegon, MI. (north of Grand Rapids)
Operating Season: May - Sept.

Michigan's Adventure is the state's only full-fledged amusement park. The park is located about 30 minutes north of Grand Rapids (or for those who don't want to look at a map: look at your hand. Where the pinky connects to your hand is roughly where Michigan Adventure is - just alittle more toward the coast!). Michigan Adventure is home to six roller coasters including the famous, and always highly rated, Shivering Timbers. In recent years the park has expanded its collection of rides by adding a train and more recently a water raft ride called Grand Rapids. During the summertime the most visitors head over to the water park, which is included in the price of admission to Michigan's Adventure, something this author really loved! It is filled with all the normal water park attractions including a large wave pool.

For more information:
- 231-766-3377
- http://www.miadventures.com

Valleyfair
Location: Shakopee, Mn.
Operating Season: May - Sept.

Valleyfair, the first park bought by Cedar Point (not yet Cedar Fair), is half of the namesake of Cedar Fair (the other half - Cedar - coming from you guessed it Cedar Point!). The park is home to 40+ rides including eight roller coasters. New for 2007 is one of the most twisted roller coasters around - Renegade! With a 91 ft. twisting first drop and speeds reaching 52 mph, Renegade is sure to be one twisted, fun, roller coaster! Other park highlights include Mad Mouse, a wild mouse roller coaster, and Wild Thing, a large hyper roller coaster. In 2006 Valleyfair followed in the footsteps of Cedar Point building a ride nearly identical to Skyhawk called Xtreme Swing (the difference - Skyhawk is two feet taller). The park also has plenty for the little ones, including a foam ball factory, a kiddie carousel and a train, and numerous other kid friendly attractions. Admission to Valleyfair also includes access to the Whitewater Country Waterpark (located in the park).

For more information:
- 800-FUN-RIDE
- http://www.valleyfair.com

World's of Fun

Location: Kansas City, MO.
Operating Season: April - Oct.

World's of Fun, with an total of 43 rides, is an amusement park located in Kansas City, MO. The park is loosely themed around the book "Around the World in Eighty Days." There are six roller coasters including the hyper coaster Mamba and the large wooden coaster Timber Wolf. Camp Snoopy features plenty for young children to do, while there are enough thrill and mild rides for anyone's taste. In 2005 the park added the Worlds of Fun village, a resort patterned after Cedar Point's Lighthouse Point. It features 22 cabins, 20 cottages, and over 80 sites for RVs.

Ocean's of Fun, which is a separate price/park from World's of Fun, is a complete waterpark. It features all your favorite water park attractions including plenty of slides, a wave pool, an adult swim-up-bar pool, and plenty of water activities for the little ones.

For more information:
- 816-454-4545
- http://www.worldsoffun.com

index

Index

Index

Index

About the Author

Andrew Hyde is a writer that has always loved amusement parks, especially Cedar Point. Ever since he could walk, Hyde has been traveling to Cedar Point. Each year his family would make their trip to the park, and while never a big fan of the rides Hyde was always fascinated by the park itself. Up until recently he was too scared to set foot on any of the parks ride then again it was not the rides drawing Hyde to the park. Hyde loved the experience and atmosphere Cedar Point provided. Hyde has been a Cedar Point season pass holder for nearly ten years and visits the park as much as he can.

Today, Andrew Hyde is pursuing a degree in communications at John Carroll University near Cleveland, Ohio, not to far from Cedar Point's sister park Geauga Lake. He still spends much of his free time writing whether it be about travel or amusement parks. He also hosts a weekly modern rock radio show on 88.7 FM in Cleveland, OH. While not at school Hyde resides in a northern Detroit suburb.

He can be contacted through ExperienceThePoint.com